Love Makes Things Happen

Love Makes Things Happen

An Invitation to Christian Living

Edited by
Jennifer Strawbridge
Jarred Mercer
and
Peter Groves

scm press

© Editors and Contributors 2022

Published in 2022 by SCM Press
Editorial office
3rd Floor, Invicta House,
108–114 Golden Lane,
London EC1Y 0TG, UK

www.scmpress.co.uk

SCM Press is an imprint of Hymns Ancient & Modern Ltd
(a registered charity)

H
Y Ancient
M &Modern
N
S

Hymns Ancient & Modern® is a registered trademark of
Hymns Ancient & Modern Ltd
13A Hellesdon Park Road, Norwich,
Norfolk NR6 5DR, UK

The Scripture quotations contained herein are from
The New Revised Standard Version of the Bible, Anglicized Edition,
Copyright © 1989, 1995 by the Division of Christian Education of the
National Council of the Churches of Christ in the United States of
America, and are used by permission. All rights reserved.

British Library Cataloguing in Publication data
A catalogue record for this book is available
from the British Library

ISBN 978-0-334-05993-6

Typeset by Regent Typesetting
Printed and bound by
CPI Group (UK) Ltd

Contents

Preface

Christianity is a lived phenomenon grounded in a call to love. As a lived, practised reality, Christianity cannot be abstract or divorced from our everyday lives. Doctrine (a word that just means 'teaching') which is separate from doing is not Christian teaching. Beginning with a focus on prayer, worship, Scripture and sacraments, *Love Makes Things Happen* explores the day-to-day experience that Christian faith is all about through the distinctive practices that manifest and depend upon Christian theology and doctrine.

The assumption in this book is that one cannot truly participate in prayer, worship, the sacraments, the reading of Scripture, or mission, in a way that is detached from the doctrine of the Trinity, or the Incarnation, or the Resurrection (whether one knows it or not). All of ordinary Christian life is a lived expression of the depths of Christian theology. The actions of Christian faith are more than just 'practical applications' of Christian teaching or theological understandings; they are the fullness of that understanding. They are doctrines that are alive, theology that breathes.

God's love is always creative – it makes things happen. It does this through the real lives of real people, among them Christian people. The actions of prayer, sacramental celebration, evangelism, justice, hospitality and public faith, which are at the heart of Christian life, are living expressions of Christian theology. As the life and teachings of Christ make clear, God loves the poor, outcast and marginalized, and that love is shared in the public square and lived out in prayer and worship. We cannot claim to be disciples without sharing that same love.

By exploring Christian doctrine as something which is done, this book examines the Christian life as it emerges from and returns to the core foundations of Christian thought. Following on from a previous collection, *Love Makes No Sense: An Invitation to Christian Theology*, the chapters which follow evidence the practicality of Christian doctrine as it naturally takes shape in the world around us and invite readers to discover that love makes things happen in the course of their Christian lives. This book does not claim to be a comprehensive introduction. It is rather, as the title suggests, an *invitation* – something to help draw the reader deeper into a living faith, with every hope that the reader continues moving far beyond these pages.

This volume is the third collection written by a group of priests connected to the St Mary Magdalen School of Theology (www.theschooloftheology.org). The School of Theology – with a mission to read, pray and teach the Christian faith – seeks to offer approachable theological teaching as it explores the central teachings of Christian faith. In what follows, readers are invited to discover anew a theology of love – God's dynamic and life-changing love – and the impact that this love has on Christian living.

List of Contributors

Simon Cuff is Vicar of St Peter de Beauvoir Town in the Diocese of London. He was formerly Lecturer in Theology at St Mellitus College and Fellow of the Centre for Theology and Community. He is a trustee of refugee charity Migrants Organise and Vice Chair of ECCR, a charity concerned with financial justice and Christian use of money.

Peter Groves is Vicar of St Mary Magdalen and Assistant Archdeacon of Oxford. He is a Senior Research Fellow in Theology at Worcester College, Oxford, where he teaches doctrine.

Jonathan Jong is Rector of Cocking with West Lavington, Bepton and Heyshott in the Diocese of Chichester. He is also an experimental psychologist and Assistant Professor at the Centre for Trust, Peace and Social Relations at Coventry University.

Melanie Marshall is Associate Priest at St Mary Magdalen, Oxford. She was previously Chaplain of Lincoln College and has taught Latin and Greek literature in Oxford for some years.

Jarred Mercer is Rector of St Paul's Episcopal Church in Newburyport, Massachusetts and formerly a chaplain and member of the Faculty of Theology and Religion at the University of Oxford, where he specialized in patristic theology.

Jennifer Strawbridge is Associate Professor in New Testament Studies at the University of Oxford and Caird Fellow in Theology at Mansfield College. She is also a theological canon at Chichester and Blackburn Cathedrals and Associate Priest at St Andrew's, Headington.

I

Love in God's Presence:
An Invitation to Prayer

JENNIFER STRAWBRIDGE

Introduction

Prayer is one of the essential elements of the Christian faith. Jesus taught his disciples to pray giving them what we now call 'The Lord's Prayer' (Matt. 6.9–13; Luke 11.2–4). Jesus also models prayers of intercession with his promise to pray for Christians when he is 'at the right hand of God' (see Rom. 8.34). Prayer is what the Apostle Paul commands us to do so that we might grow into the full stature of Christ (1 Thess. 5.17; Eph. 4.13) and what he too models through his prayer for his colleagues and communities night and day (Phil. 1.4). Prayer is even what the Spirit does on our behalf, offering 'sighs too deep for words' (Rom. 8.26).

But prayer is easy to take for granted. If you are a Christian, you might assume that you know how to pray or that everyone else seems to know and so you fake it until you make it. For some, prayer is a kind of 'spiritual Father Christmas business' (Williams) where we make a list and if we have been good, some of the petitions might be granted. For others, prayer is open and spontaneous and we speak as the Spirit moves us. And for some, prayer is set, built upon the words written in a book of common prayer and often part of a service said every morning and evening. If you are not religious, prayer may seem rather pointless and an exercise of speaking our needs into the ether; a way of making ourselves feel better in difficult situations, but it doesn't actually do anything.

As Christians, however, prayer determines how we live our lives. This belief isn't new but goes all the way back to the earliest Christians. The command to pray and examples of prayer are found throughout our scriptures and across our tradition and are 'multi-faceted, profound, and without true precedent or analogy' (Hurtado, p. 35). The Gospels and earliest Christian writers assume that prayer is a part of life, not simply what happens when Christians gather together (and how much more has this been true in the time of Covid?). God is always present and always active in all that we do, and prayer is simply acknowledging this truth. It is, in many ways, like breathing. But, as a wise monk clarifies, 'breathing is never just one more task on our list of things to do. It is essential to life; without it we die. Prayer, like breathing, is essential to our life in God. Without it, our spiritual lives cannot be sustained' (Vryhof).

So how do we respond to God in prayer? How might prayer infuse our lives? This chapter explores such questions through Scripture, looking to Jesus as a model for prayer, and examining the ways that prayer can be communal and solitary, gourmet or very simple, and how it helps us to engage with the joys and sorrows of our transitory lives.

What does it mean to pray? Looking to Jesus as our model

One of the biggest challenges of prayer is that our minds are constantly on the go, working overtime as we engage with the demands and expectations placed upon us each day, perhaps as a parent or carer or as part of our attempt to balance the work and non-work-related parts of our day. We are distracted by the things we really ought to be doing, by overflowing inboxes, by stacks of paper, by a pastoral concern, and by the demands of family and friends. More than these distractions, we are also not very good with engaging silence. For some of us, space for silence might be part of our spiritual discipline. For others, we might not ever have intentionally created space in our lives for silence with God. Rather, as we stop to pray and as we focus on God in our day, we find we are distracted, exhausted, a bit unsure how to proceed, and possibly anxious about what we might encounter in this space.

The Gospels are a help and encouragement in the task of stopping to pray, offering a healthy number of examples for how we might prepare ourselves for time dedicated to God. Perhaps you can relate to the disciples in Mark's Gospel, for example, who are so excited about their work and all they are doing in the world. We are told, 'The apostles gathered around Jesus and reported all they had done and taught. He said to them, "Come away to a deserted place all by yourselves and rest a while." For many were coming and going ... And they went away in the boat to a deserted place by themselves' (Mark 6.30–32).

Mark essentially gives us an account of the beginning of one of the first Christian retreats. Even in their enthusiasm for their ministry and their work, even when people gathered in great numbers, even with demands all around them, the disciples needed to step away to a deserted place with Jesus in order better to live into their life of faith. And they do so time and again, even in the midst of busyness, even in the midst of many demands on their time and their prayers.

This story from Mark's Gospel is packed with nuggets we can glean for our own approach to prayer. Within this narrative we first have a situation that many of us know all too well, the moment when the disciples have been so busy and excited by their work that they haven't even had time to eat – and here we can also read, pray – and so Jesus invites them away to a deserted place. This passage affirms that there are times when our lives will be so full and demanding that we will have to be incredibly intentional about carving out space for prayer. We will have to pay attention to those moments when Jesus is calling us away to pray so that we can recharge and refresh and then reengage with energy and grace. Notice as well that this calling isn't necessarily to private prayer, but is Jesus with all the disciples, perhaps encouraging us to hold onto those moments of prayer with our family or within the setting of a community. Jesus and the disciples model both a call away from busyness so that we don't neglect our relationship with God and a call away from busyness so that we don't neglect our relationships with those nearest and dearest, those who support us and who rely on us for support.

Of course, this kind of prayer is difficult. As we find throughout the Gospels, as soon as Jesus tries to step away for prayer, people keep pursuing him and making demands of him. But, curiously, this doesn't stop him trying to pray. Both Mark and Luke tell us in their Gospels that 'In the morning, while it was still very dark, he got up and went out to a deserted place, and there he prayed. And Simon and his companions hunted for him. When they found him, they said to him, "Everyone is searching for you"' (Mark 1.35–37; cf. Luke 4.42).

This second story shows us that even when there was a lot to do and people needed him, Jesus took time apart. He didn't go off to a solitary place only when all of the demands on him had ceased. Jesus went off to a solitary place because of the essential need for prayer despite all the things that had to be done. In a way, we are all spiritual introverts like our Lord, who while energized by the crowds and time with his disciples, also still needs space to recharge before carrying on. Even Jesus needs time to feed himself in communion with God. So too we need our time alone with God, away from the crowds to recharge our spiritual batteries. People won't always like it when we step away for time with God, nor will they always understand. The Gospels grasp this too. The Gospels don't ignore the reality that the outside world often manages to break in. This is what makes the balance of prayer so difficult, because while it would be nice if we always operated out of a place of prayer and calmness, the reality is that this is impossible much of the time.

The essential thing that we learn from Jesus and his own practices of prayer is intentionality. How do we ensure that in the midst of the demands on us and the busyness that surrounds us, we don't forget to pray?

Boundary crossing in prayer: intercession

The kind of prayer that we most often pray, whether we know it or not, is a prayer of intercession. Intercession is simply the act of taking to God our own needs or the needs of another. Intercession is what we do when we pray for the health of a friend or family member or when we pray for peace at a particularly anxious time. Intercession isn't just a list of the needs of the world but brings others, in love, before God. Jesus himself is the model for this prayer, seated at God's right hand and praying for us (Heb. 7.25). Here, Jesus isn't just talking to God about us, but carrying us in his heart to God.

What this looks like for us and how we model Jesus' prayer in our lives might vary. Sometimes we might be like the sightless Bartimaeus who cries out to Jesus for mercy (Matt. 20.30; Mark 10.47; Luke 18.38). At other times, we might be like the Syrophoenician woman begging Jesus to heal her daughter (Matt. 15.22–28; Mark 7.25–30) or the Centurion who begs Jesus to heal his servant (Matt. 8.5; Luke 7.2–10). Jesus' first miracle in John's Gospel at the wedding at Cana also gives us a sense of what a prayer of intercession might look like in our lives.

In this story, we have a rather desperate situation at a wedding: the wine has run out. Mary, Jesus' mother, knows that he is the one who can bring some resolution to the situation. So she approaches him and tells him the situation in only a few words ('They have no wine') and Jesus, while at first being rather dismissive, performs a miracle and the bridegroom's reputation is saved. Here Mary's actions teach us about intercession. She sees a situation which she knows is difficult. It's not even really her problem – it is the bridegroom's problem – but she intercedes on his behalf, we might say, and brings the situation to Jesus. In the process, she crosses a boundary in the ancient world between women and men, she makes a demand, she petitions God the Son on behalf of another.

Mary's actions are at the heart of what intercessory prayer is. Intercession prays across boundaries, engages with situations where no one is totally sure what they need or want except that they know they need prayer. This prayer carries that person to God and brings before God from a place of love and compassion those who long to be healed and made whole. Pray for my sick aunt, or my dying pet, or my terrible job, or for football on Saturday are all things we might be asked to do as a Christian. Prayer interacts intimately with the nitty gritty of our days and can be about something as simple as wine at a wedding. And yet, as the Gospel story is clear, Jesus doesn't dismiss Mary's request as a terrible idea or part of her personal agenda, but he listens and he responds.

Anne Lamott, a wonderful spiritual writer, in her wisdom writes that there are really only three kinds of prayers that we pray: help, thanks and wow. The prayer at Cana, and prayers of intercessions for ourselves and for others, are quintessential 'help' prayers. Such prayers involve asking for the unknown and risking being wrong. This prayer doesn't have to be dramatic and it doesn't have to be formal. It can be as simple as a prayer when an ambulance or a hearse drive by, or as basic as that at our bedside or before a meal.

Two models for prayer: Mary and Martha

Speaking of meals, we find that another Gospel story in a more intimate setting than a large wedding but also involving a meal speaks to us about how we are to pray and the impact of our prayer. This is the story of Mary and Martha that we find in Luke's Gospel (snippets of which are also in John's narrative).

In Luke 10.38–42 we find written, 'Now as they went on their way, he entered a certain village, where a woman named Martha welcomed him into her home. She had a sister named Mary, who sat at the Lord's feet and listened to what he was saying. But Martha was distracted by her many tasks; so she came to him and asked, "Lord, do you not care that my sister has left me to do all the work by myself? Tell her then to help me." But the Lord answered her, "Martha, Martha, you are worried and distracted by many things; there is need of only one thing. Mary has chosen the better part, which will not be taken away from her.'

Here we have two different kinds of prayer, although one isn't always acknowledged as such: Mary, who sits in silence with the Lord, listening to all that God has to say and Martha, distracted by many tasks, complaining to the Lord about her situation. While Martha is scolded by the Lord, both Mary and Martha are offering prayer.

The first kind of prayer – Mary's prayer – could fall into any of the three categories offered by Anne Lamott: help, thanks or wow. This kind of prayer, offered in silence, isn't just for those who are on retreat but speaks to the silence that will be part of all our prayers at some point in our lives. We might sit in silence with the Lord because we are listening for what is next and seeking God's guidance and clarity. We might sit in silence with the Lord because we are so in awe of how good God is and how much we have been given even when we don't deserve it; even when our prayer life might be terrible. We might sit in silence with the Lord because the situation we face, because those we are with are struggling and words cannot begin to bring comfort. We might sit in silence with the Lord because we have nothing to say, we are done, empty, or even angry and giving God the silent treatment. God can deal with all of these situations and all of these situations are prayer. Silence is especially difficult when it is so easy to avoid with all of the distractions and diversions that the world offers as well as our own inability to stop talking when we are anxious, and so it is all the more important that like Mary we take the time to be with God in silence, seeking, listening, discerning, and even just stopping for a moment when we can't find the words to pray.

But then there are also the times when we need Martha's prayer, when we simply need to complain to God. This is the kind of prayer that comes from our anxiety and our judgement of another – the kind of prayer like Martha's which says: Why don't you do something, God and why don't you do something with this other person and make them help me? These are also incredibly important prayers as they will save us from bitterness, resentment and judgement. There are times that we will need to express our incredulity to God, our anger to God, because there is no one else we can do this with. Working through things with God – be it a breakup, a death, a health scare, anxiety – expressing our difficulty and grief in prayer, is crucial and an important prayer we must pray.

Within this story we notice both Mary's silence and Martha's anxiety and busyness and often prioritize Mary as praying the 'right' way. But as much as Martha gets a bad rap, she still seeks the Lord and speaks to him in the midst of her busyness and judgement. She also listens enough that she can be chastened by him and yet doesn't walk away. Even when the worst thing happens, and her brother Lazarus dies, Martha doesn't turn away but keeps seeking her Lord. Here we see that while we are tempted constantly to be busy, to allow our work, as it will, to spill into all aspects of our lives, even in the busyness and the frustrations and even the tragedies of life, Mary and Martha's examples encourage us to be persistent in our prayers and to seek the Lord.

Prayer is as simple and as difficult as putting ourselves near God, with God, in a time of quietness every day. Prayer is putting ourselves with God just as we are, with our complaints and silences and thanksgivings, in the feebleness of our concentration, in our lack of warmth and desire, not trying to manufacture pious thoughts or phrases, as Mary and Martha so wonderfully demonstrate. It's not about doing certain devotional exercises – though the rhythm and familiar nature of the daily office can certainly help in difficult times – but by daring to be yourself, completely yourself, as you reach out to God.

Prayer in community

Many of the approaches to prayer touched on thus far concern our private, individual prayers: prayer on behalf of another or ourselves, prayer that takes risks, prayer that speaks to anxiety or grief, prayer that is help, thanks and wow. All of these kinds of prayer are essential to our lives and our being. But sometimes, we also need to pray with another and within a community. In a way, we are all both introverts and extroverts when it comes to prayer: at times we need space and silence in order to recharge and at other times we need people and community to do so. To sustain us and direct our hearts to God, we need both.

Communal prayer, of course, takes many forms, from the Eucharist whenever it happens to other set services within our communities, be they within the walls of the church or at the blessing of the summer fair or the local fire engines or even online. Prayer is not only about discerning how you will create space away from the mess and in moments of quiet and intimacy; it is also about being able to be prayerful in the midst of the chaos and the mess and with a gathered community, the place where incarnation really happens. And there is really no better example of this than the Eucharist, gathered around God's table and breaking bread together.

So we read the intimate account in Matthew's Gospel:

When it was evening, he took his place with the twelve; and while they were eating, he said, 'Truly I tell you, one of you will betray me.' And they became greatly distressed and began to say to him one after another, 'Surely not I, Lord?' He answered, 'The one who has dipped his hand into the bowl with me will betray me' ... While they were eating, Jesus took a loaf of bread, and after blessing it he broke it, gave it to the disciples, and said, 'Take, eat; this is my body.' Then he took a cup, and after giving thanks he gave it to them, saying, 'Drink from it, all of you; for this is my blood of the covenant, which is poured out for many for the forgiveness of sins. I tell you, I will never again drink of this fruit of the vine until that day when I drink it new with you in my Father's kingdom.' When they had sung the hymn, they went out to the Mount of Olives. (Matt. 26.20–30)

The model of communal prayer that we find in this scene is twofold. On the one hand, communal prayer is intimate and connects us directly to God, so close that we know God's presence with us in community. In this kind of communal prayer, we find ourselves invited into this space to know God's presence and to enter more deeply into relationship with our Lord who is present to us in the breaking of bread and in the prayers. In a very practical way, the Eucharist serves as a moment when we step away from the world and enter into one extended prayer: a prayer that begins with the hearing of the Word and lifting our hearts to God, receiving the nourishment of the sacrament, and then being dismissed to go out and serve. As the Gospel passage concludes, 'when they had sung the hymn, they went out ...'. The Eucharist is inherently communal even if only two are gathered. Communal worship can replenish our spiritual reserves.

The other model of communal prayer we encounter in this story from Matthew's Gospel picks up on those times when we approach our Lord in doubt and even great distress. These are the times when we find ourselves questioning our calling, our faith, and we ask alongside the disciples: 'Is it I, Lord'? Matthew's Gospel demonstrates in this moment the particular way that communal prayer can draw us back to God in prayer. Even as the disciples doubt themselves and their commitment to their Lord, they do so within his presence and his earshot. This is especially powerful for those times when the words of prayer that we pray together lift to God the words that, in difficult times, we cannot pray on our own. One essential element of communal prayer – be that the daily office, the Eucharist, or any communal worship – is the rootedness of this prayer in Scripture, in the corporate prayer of the Church and in something beyond ourselves. This does not mean that we

are delegating our prayer life to someone else, but rather that
at times, many times, the prayer of the wider church and of our
community can hold and sustain us.

Times of communal prayer can sustain us when times of private prayer cannot and throughout our lives different kinds of
prayer and different ways of praying will hold us in times of
greatest joy and deepest doubt and struggle. At times prayer
can feel like a burden – be it the morning when you just want to
sleep, the time when you would rather be at home in pyjamas,
the busy days when even a five-minute break feels impossible,
and those times when you simply cannot pray. And this, in
particular, is where communal prayer is essential, because there
will be times when you will feel intimately connected with God
and there will be times when you will not, and those times
are when we need communal prayer the most. In communal
prayer, the community prays as we stand with them and helps
us realize we are not alone in our prayer but being carried by
those who have gone before and those who stand with us and
surround us in prayer.

Our introverted and extroverted needs in prayer will ebb and
flow throughout our lives. Sometimes our private prayer will
sustain us and at other times the prayers of the community will
pray for us when we cannot pray alone. Both kinds of prayer –
introverted and extroverted, private and communal – are part
of our lives as Christians. We are called then to be aware of how
each kind of prayer feeds us, sustains us and works together in
our lives. We are also called, as much as we are able, to notice
when we are distracted and disturbed and unable to pray in a
particular way or setting. When (not if) such times occur in our
lives, one of the most important things we can do for our life
and our faith is to make sure we don't fall into the trap of not
praying, of feeling guilty, or of becoming cynical, but rather to
try different approaches to recharge and start again with God.
For some, it might be a trusted passage of Scripture, for others,
the words of the Eucharist, and for others, it may be words of
encouragement from a trusted friend or mentor that draws us
back and keeps us rooted in hope and in prayer.

Final reflections on prayer

Prayer is a gift from God as we respond to God's love and presence in our lives and our world. Our life in prayer will rarely be perfect and, as in life, will have its highs and lows and times of feast and famine. Prayer rarely goes according to our plans, but such a reality is actually good news. It is good news because of the truth that even when we are not as faithful or as prayerful as we think we should be, and even when we fall short of our expectations and those of others, God is faithful. As the Apostle Paul writes to the Thessalonians, 'The one who calls you is faithful, and he will do this' (1 Thess. 5.24). God is faithful and this reality alone is one of the greatest sources of support in prayer.

The God who calls us is faithful and we are called to pray each and every day, standing before God with or without words, holding ourselves and those whom we love in our hearts and offering them to God. Every single day we have the opportunity to make space for prayer. A dear friend who happens to be a monk once described this choice with the image of God as a beloved pet labrador. He says that every morning when we wake up, God is dancing by our bed, excited for the new day and wondering what we will do together, and how it is that God will surprise us and delight us and delight in us. And more often than not, we leave God there, beside our bed while we go about our day and then at its end, if we aren't too tired, we report back to God about how it went and ask for God's help with the next day. Without prayer, we don't invite or expect God to journey with us and we don't allow space for God to surprise us with mercy and grace and love. But God is faithful and whether we know it or not, whether it feels like it or not, whether our prayer life is faithful or not, God does not leave or forsake us, but endures with us.

While our prayer may not be perfect, another aspect of prayer is that our prayer life will also never be complete. This both is a terrifying and comforting thought because it means that we will never have it all figured out and that we must continue to grow in our prayer, go deeper in our prayer even as we endure moments of doubt, of being overwhelmed, of joy, and moments of thinking that we and not God are in control of a situation. Perhaps one of the best examples of the way our prayer life can and will change is illustrated in one final Gospel story, this time from John:

> When it was evening on that day, the first day of the week, and the doors of the house where the disciples had met were locked for fear of the Jews, Jesus came and stood among them and said, 'Peace be with you.' After he said this, he showed them his hands and his side. Then the disciples rejoiced when they saw the Lord. Jesus said to them again, 'Peace be with you. As the father has sent me, so I send you.' When he had said this, he breathed on them and said to them, 'Receive the Holy Spirit…'. (John 20.19–22)

Throughout their lives, the disciples have been called to do amazing things with Jesus, they have fed people and offered healing and comfort, they have interceded on behalf of others and they have complained bitterly about their situation, and yet in spite of all of this, we find them locked away for fear. They have lost their confidence and their trust. The way of prayer that has always worked for them, namely spending time with Jesus himself as he teaches them to pray, is gone now that Jesus is gone, so it feels. But suddenly Jesus appears and not only are they filled with joy, but Jesus offers them peace and the encouragement they need to go out and be the rock of the church, the ones who feed the sheep and tend the lambs, who proclaim the gospel and offer healing. Their prayer continues to evolve and deepen even after Jesus' death, as they embrace a new way of praying with the help of the Holy Spirit. And while our circumstances are perhaps not this dramatic, this story encompasses much of our prayer lives as well.

There will be times when we, like the disciples throughout the Gospels, will be excited and full of joy and there will be moments when we lose confidence and close ourselves behind a door in fear and anxiety. In both of these moments, we are promised that there is always the hope of resurrection and always the possibility of God offering us a new way to pray, to be in relationship and to be within our community. May we, with those first disciples, receive the Spirit of God, the peace that only God can give, and get on with the work we are called to do.

Questions for further reflection

• How do you pray when you are alone? How about when you are with a community?
• How does prayer sustain you in the joys and sorrows of life?
• How do the examples we have from Jesus, praying with his disciples, praying alone on a mountain, and offering the last supper, infuse and inform your own life of prayer?

Bibliography

Larry W. Hurtado, 2014, 'The Place of Jesus in Earliest Christian Prayer and its Import for Early Christian Identity', in Reidar Hvalvik and Karl Olav Sandnes (eds), *Early Christian Prayer and Identity Formation*, Tübingen: Mohr Siebeck, pp. 35–56.
Anne Lamott, 2013, *Help, Thanks, Wow: The Three Essential Prayers*, London: Hodder & Stoughton.
David Vryhof SSJE, 2009, 'Prayer and Life', https://www.ssje.org/2009/03/24/prayer-and-life/ (accessed 29.12.2021).
Rowan Williams, 2009, 'Growing in Prayer: What the Saints tell us about the Spiritual Journey, Lecture 1', https://www.themathesontrust.org/library/growing-in-prayer (accessed 29.12.2021).

Further reading

Wendell Berry, 1998, *A Timbered Choir: The Sabbath Poems 1979–1997*, Washington, DC: Counterpoint.
Margaret Guenther, 2006, *At Home in the World: A Rule of Life for the Rest of Us*, New York: Church Publishing Incorporated.
Martin Warner, 2005, *The Habit of Holiness: Daily Prayer*, London: Morehouse Publishing.

2

Love in Offering:
An Invitation to Worship

JARRED MERCER

Introduction: what is worship?

Worship is not something easy to define. We often think of
worship as synonymous with the liturgy or particular 'worship'
services in 'houses of worship'. Some even refer to particular
parts of church services as worship – the music, for instance.
Someone might read from Scripture, someone else preach a
sermon and lead other parts of the service, and then someone
else or a group of people will ascend to the front of the building to lead the congregation in 'worship'. 'Worship' today
even designates a style of music – there is classical, folk, rock,
jazz and, apparently, worship music. Others will use the word
to refer to an inward disposition towards God, a humility of
spirit, a prayerful acknowledgement that God is God and we
are not. On some level, these are all legitimate uses of the word
(some more than others, I would argue!), but not one of them,
or even all of them together, will satisfy the question 'What
is worship?' But I bring this variety of meanings, which is by
no means an exhaustive list, to our minds because the breadth
of our understanding of worship tells us something about the
nature of worship itself. In other words, the lack of definition
is an essential revelation of what worship truly is – it is, in a
sense, boundless, because it touches everything.

Our habitual tendency to pin worship down to particular

aspects of liturgical practice or to modern brandings of largely derivative and highly commercialized melodies leads us very quickly to turn inward. Worship too easily becomes about us rather than God. So, we can speak of 'not getting anything out of the worship' on Sundays as if worship was a consumer product meant to fill and satisfy us rather than the opposite – an act of giving ourselves away as an offering. Or people easily and naturally refer to particular 'styles' of worship – high church or low church, traditional or contemporary – as 'not for me', as if worship was meant to be 'for me' or 'about me' at all.

But it isn't. It's not about me. It's about God, and that reorients us from an inward to an outward motion in worship. If worship is about God, it should turn us outward beyond ourselves, not further into ourselves, and in doing so it reveals to us who we really are – what it means to be a human person – by bringing us into the life we are meant to live: not an inward-facing life, but a God-ward facing life. This means that worship, though it isn't about us, does change us. It does form, educate and shape us in a new direction and transform our entire vision of the world, God and ourselves. In other words, turning towards God in worship reveals to ourselves that we are ourselves, and reveals to the world that it is indeed the world – loved, embraced, cherished and pursued – by revealing God for who God is.

And this determines, or at least it should determine, what that smaller definition of worship looks like – what we do when gathered as a community for worship. But, in turn, what we do when gathered is valid only insofar as it reaches beyond the gathering to that revealing of ourselves to ourselves and the world to the world by revealing God in Christ.

Rowan Williams said of Christians joining together to celebrate the Eucharist, the central act of Christian worship, that 'they allow themselves to be interrogated by the story of Christ's self-sacrifice, to be questioned as to whether their present lives are recognizably linked with Christ's and to be reconnected with the story of Christ's death and resurrection by the renewing gift of the Holy Spirit' ('Worship'). This 'being interrogated' by the story means the story isn't over. We find ourselves wrapped up in it, in dialogue with it, as we are transformed by and into it by participating in Christ's sacrifice in the Eucharist. The liturgical expression of our life together, the gathered, worshipping community, is a microcosm of our whole being – an interrogation of our lives that, sometimes slowly over time, sometimes with pain and difficulty, and always with joy and fullness, pulls the truth out of us – the truth about God, the world and ourselves – and orients our living towards that truth. In other words, the life interrogated is the life transformed. The life that enters the story of Christ's self-giving love in the eucharistic fellowship of the Church continues to live that story, giving itself away with all the risk and uncertainty that entails, trusting in what it has received. Worship is our whole story. It is the entirety of our lives.

The offering of worship and holistic transformation

In his book *Ancient Christian Worship* (pp. 2–3), Andrew McGowan points to the use of the word 'worship' in the 1549 Book of Common Prayer marriage service. We can see this in the 1662 BCP as well, still in use in many English churches today. The 'Liturgy of Holy Matrimony' in the 1662 Book of Common Prayer includes these words, retained from the 1549 book, during the giving of the wedding ring: 'With this ring I thee wed, with my body I thee worship, and with all my worldly goods I thee endow'. Here the meaning of the word worship does not refer to some special devotion to the spouse, but to the giving of a token, and to the sharing of possessions: it is an offering and a gift.

This understanding of worship as offering, as the giving of a gift, spreads far beyond holy matrimony. In fact, the word *leitourgia*, or liturgy, means 'service', or 'work of (or for) the people'. The word originally referred to public service and almsgiving – care for the poor and ethical, even political action in the world. The liturgy involves the communal act of worship

and prayer that is the source of all other activity and movement of the Church in service to others – particularly in the
Eucharist. But the liturgy, the *leitourgia*, only refers to such
communal worship insofar as that worship is the source and
spring of the whole Christian life; only insofar as 'worship'
means not just what we do as we gather together for prayer,
learning, singing, and so forth – though it certainly includes
that – but the whole lived life of the Church as an offering
of love and service to God and to the world around us. We
go to worship 'services' so that we can become the sent ones
who leave the comfort of our church buildings to undertake
the risk of 'service', becoming an offering for a hurting world.
It is no coincidence that the closing words of the traditional
Latin mass are '*Ite, missa est*': quite literally, 'Go, the dismissal
is made'. Our communal worship is only true worship when
it refuses to end there. There is a sense in which the ultimate
liturgical act is to walk out of the church and continue to give
ourselves away in love and service.

Worship is the entire Christian life – our deepest beliefs and
aspirations, both our embodied practice and inward faith –
our entire relation to and response to God. It is the gift of our
whole selves.

But our shared identity through prayer and liturgical practice (what we typically mean by worship) is not divorced from
this wholeness; it works to both represent and to sustain and
create this holistic vision of our life with one another and
before God. It gives us a certain posture, a relation towards
God, and opens up our humanity to our ultimate end and fullness. And this worshipping posture is a posture of *offering*.
Worship is self-gift – a de-centring of ourselves in adoration
of God. And the act of adoration – gathered in communal liturgy, offered in the Eucharist, gifted through our life of private
prayer, shared in humble service to the poor – is itself the self-
gift of love with which worship is concerned. William Temple
put it this way: 'Worship is the submission of all our nature
to God. It is the quickening of the conscience by his holiness;
the nourishment of mind with his truth; the purifying of the

imagination by his beauty; the opening of the heart to his love; the surrender of will to his purpose – and all of this gathered up in adoration, the most selfless emotion of which our nature is capable.' He continues to say worship is the 'chief remedy' of self-centredness, which is the source of our sin (Temple, p. 67).

Adoration, true worship, de-centres the self and turns us outward. As such, it is deeply transformative, it is an act of repentance as it changes our minds about God, ourselves, and others, and it is holistic as an offering of our whole lives to God and others – opposing our tendencies of turning inward in the self-idolatry we call sin. This is a far cry from the often-sentimentalized expressions of worship that revolve around filling oneself up, satisfying personal preferences, and often comfortingly confirming one's own ideas about who God is or what God is doing in our lives and our world. Yes, we join in and confess our faith together in word and deed, but genuine worship should also consist of being confronted with things that call us to such repentance and change that we find it almost impossible, at least initially, to lend our 'Amen'. As Richard Rohr has said: 'Before the truth "sets you free", it tends to make you miserable' (Rohr, p. 74).

True worship should consist of a holy disturbance. It disturbs our vision of ourselves and our world and opens us up to God's surprising work in our lives. And all of this is radically discomforting. If we have perceived worship to be an event of corporate gathering that satisfies our own preferences – be they 'styles' of liturgy or music or notions of a self-gratifying sense of comfort or fulfilment – I'm afraid we've missed the point. Perhaps if we are to explore the true nature of worship, we should examine the moments of holy conflict that arise in our prayer, our listening, our liturgical life as the Church. Where are the points where our instinct is to join St Peter: 'No! not I, Jesus!' only to find ourselves later by the fireside in complete shock at ourselves? These are key moments in our worship, or at least, key turning points where we are confronted with the choice to choose right worship – that adoration that turns us outward beyond ourselves – or to choose self-exaltation and idolatry.

'With my body I thee worship'. Worship is embodied and holistic. It involves our whole lives. Yes, what we do communally in the liturgy. Yes, the state of our minds in prayer. But also, daily expressions of living – from mundane kindnesses, truth telling, and care for others, to grand movements of mercy on a global scale. And this is always transformative. Worship always involves change and renewal. It is a work of repentance that leads to offering, a labour of transformation in our lives that always seeks to move outward towards the transformation of others.

Homo adorans: worshipping in the right direction

Worship is not only the entire Christian life, but all human life. God does not need our worship. Our worship is entirely unnecessary for God. God exists in eternal adoration, in the eternal self-gift of offering we call worship already as Father, Son and Holy Spirit. This is what it means to be God. Worship is, however, necessary for us. Worship is, in fact, how we become *us*, it makes us human. To be fully human, to live into the fullness of who we are created to be, is to participate in the life of the Triune God – to, in Christ and by the Spirit, enter and share in that life of offering. To be a fully human person is to respond to the invitation to join in the life of eternal, holy adoration of the Trinity. In other words, though God does not need our worship of God, *we do*. Worship is what makes us who we are, to turn outward in adoration, to participate in the life of the self-giving love of God is what we are made for, it is definitive of human life. We are, as it has often been said, not just *homo sapiens* – knowledgeable or reasoning humans, but *homo adorans* – worshipping ones.

One might contend with this by saying, 'but I know all kinds of people who do not worship God in any way, and they are still very much human!' Perhaps that's true, but because we are necessarily worshipping beings, because worship is at the core of who we are, just because we might not be offering our worship, our adoration, our reaching out beyond ourselves to God, does not mean we are not always worshipping something. We are always desiring, always directing ourselves towards something, always reaching out, always worshipping – we are just not always worshipping in the right direction. We may not think we serve or believe in a pantheon of gods, but perhaps we do. We may not have Ares or Mars, but we have war, a terrifyingly central god in our world. We may not pray to Eros or Cupid, but the idols of finding our self-worth in intimacy and relationships are as looming as ever. We may not worship Hermes or Mercury, but commerce and greed are surely the greatest gods of our time.

The call of the Church is to show one another and the world what right worship, what loving in the right direction really looks like, just as Christ has done. The Letter to the Hebrews describes this vividly. When Christ came as our high priest and offered himself as the sacrifice for us, he, the author says, 'purif[ies] our conscience from dead works to worship the living God!' (Heb. 9.14). In other words, worship of the living God is not just some feel-good, praise singalong service on a Sunday, it is the liberation from and the opposite of dead works. Worship, the effect of Christ's self-gift of love to us, is living works, works of life, a life that works for the blessing of the world. This is what true worship looks like: to love the Lord your God with all your heart, soul, mind, and strength, and to love your neighbour as yourself, to use Jesus' own summary of all right living.

And the connection Jesus makes here is extraordinary: there is no true love of God without love of others. That selfless love of neighbour as ourselves is the natural outgrowth of true and genuine worship – of loving God with our whole selves, of that continual gaze of adoration, moving outward beyond ourselves towards the triune life of God.

And this insoluble connection between love of God and neighbour, between worship of God and the blessing of others, further points to the eternal reality of God the Trinity living as adoring, worshipping, self-gift. Only a God who is endless overflowing love makes love the greatest commandment. Only a God who is endless overflowing love makes a command so sweet, makes the way of Christ – which isn't always easy, which involves great risk (love is always risk) – more desirable than anything else we could possibly imagine. And if we're truly to worship, to hear, to follow, this God of love, if we are to share in that love, we too must become love overflowing.

Our liturgy, our communal worship together, trains us up in this life of offering and directs our love – this whole life of worship. As we bring all that we are to the Eucharist and give ourselves away, joining with Christ's offering on the cross, and as we become one by sharing in the one bread (1 Cor. 10.17) – laying down our selfishness and narcissism for unity, equality, inclusion and reconciliation, we're enabled to live this reconciliation, inclusion, equality and unity in the whole of our lives beyond the walls of the church building. In that gathered space we learn who we are, we are becoming ourselves as Christ's people, so that we can live as our true selves everywhere else we go – loving God and loving neighbour, living lives that worship in the right direction.

Learning worship: the school of the liturgy

This 'training ground' of the liturgy means that our communal worship is also educative. When we gather, we are not just worshipping but *learning* worship. This is one reason why both the shape and content of our corporate worship matters so much: how we worship together on a Sunday morning or throughout the week, how we pray, move, kneel, stand, eat and drink, preach and hear, make peace with one another and offer our lives to God and each other shapes how we live when we leave the gathering. The Eucharist shapes eucharistic lives.

As worship reorients our entire vision of the world and ourselves before God, our ritual life in liturgy and sacrament works creatively in our life of worship. In the liturgical and sacramental life of the Church we are being enculturated, trained to see the world in a certain way, from a certain vantage point, and to live towards a certain *end* or purpose. We are being given a new interpretation of the world – entering the story of our lives, the ongoing story of God, through a different door than those offered in our lives outside the grounding of the Church's liturgical life. It is a gathering up of our whole lives and the entirety of the world around us and bringing it before God as an offering, acknowledging God's reign over all of it; a reign that rests on God's own offering of self-giving love. And this changes something in us, it hones our practice of offering ourselves in love; trains us up in love of God and neighbour; shapes our lives for more offering, more worship, more living in the way of Jesus Christ.

This being the case – the beautiful, purposeful and earth-shattering case – if our communal acts of worship are mostly about personal 'experience' (a horrid word when modified by 'worship'!), mostly about 'taking' or receiving rather than giving, mostly about the honour of ourselves, or worse, the honour of the dynamic, charismatic leader up front, we have to ask ourselves – what are we being educated into? For what sort of life are we being trained? What sort of people are we practising to become? Because the question is not '*Is* our worship forming and shaping us into the kind of church, the kind of people, that we are?', the question is '*In what direction* is our worship forming and shaping us?' because it most certainly is doing the work of forming and shaping.

The educative role of our liturgy and communal worship is, of course, a secondary effect. God is the focus, not our education. But, in our experience, this is impossible to parse out or separate. Drawing near to God and learning ourselves through worship are inseparable. The shape and content of our worship is important because it reveals what we believe about God and leads us into ourselves. And this is true of *all* our worship – whether right worship of God or misplaced worship of other things. Our embodied practices, our lived lives, are much more formative than pure ideas or beliefs. As James K. A. Smith points out, long before we structure a theology, we sing God's praises. Before we form a system of ethics, we give and receive forgiveness. Before we seek to make sense of Christ's humanity and divinity, we receive the body of Christ in the Eucharist. Before we think about God, we pray to God – 'That's the kind of animals we are, first and foremost: loving, desiring, affective, liturgical animals who, for the most part, don't inhabit the world as thinkers or cognitive machines' (Smith, pp. 33–4).

And this can be said of everything in life. I could watch every football highlight in the world and become quite knowledgeable in some ways. But if I never get out on the pitch to even kick a ball, I will never truly know the game. The *doing* is the key, and the true teacher in the end. In the same way, if we approach and express our faith in worship as a cognitive exercise that is not understood within the rhythm and movement of the practices within which it is shaped, it is difficult to see how such a faith will touch down fully in our everyday lives. We are in danger of being the 'footballer' who has watched all the highlights and read all the stats but never kicked a ball.

Liturgy and worship primarily concerned with intellectual and rationalist 'messages', absorbing information through disembodied spirituality, risks revealing a God who is not so present in our lived reality, in the stuff of our life and world, but is rather a distant figure somewhere other, somewhere heavenly beyond. Embodied worship in which we touch, taste, smell, hear, move, reveals God among us in our everyday reality, and trains us up to be with God in all our mundane motions and to recognize God among us in the motions of others.

The God who feeds you at the altar is the God who feeds the poor, the God who meets you in water and wine, in oil and touch, is the God who meets you in the streets and the workplace, the God who is at home in all creation. And worship of this God can be as simple as making a home there too. Worship is to be at home with God in the world.

Worship as offering: being at home with God

This brings us back to where we began: worship as the gift of our whole selves. Because meeting God in the world, that outward-facing attention and adoration to the God who shows up in our lives and world, is always an act of offering. So, while worship educates and transforms us – makes us who we are – it is never about or for us or about what we can gain from it. It is just the opposite: it is losing everything.

Worship cannot be treated like another product or utility in our endless cycle of consumerism. God's economy works differently than ours. And entering into this economy of grace through the offering, the sacrifice of worship, is to live in conscious critique and protest of our consumer culture. But in this giving ourselves away we are paradoxically truly filled. The offering of the work of human hands returns to us as the bread of life. The offering of the fruit of the vine returns to us as the cup of salvation. Worship creates a different sort of society, a culture of self-gift that opposes our culture of production and consumption.

This makes worship – this great act of de-centring the self – a life not only of offering to God but also a gift to others, an offering to and for the world. *Ite, missa est*, remember – the ultimate liturgical act of walking out of the church and continuing to give ourselves away. When we offer ourselves to God in worship we bring the whole world with us, and in turn become a gift from God to the world.

The fact that worship is decidedly and definitively not about ourselves is precisely how worship renews and transforms us and is our true vocation – turning our gaze from ourselves to love of God and neighbour. It is the worship of the self, self-idolatry, that creates and resources the breakdown of human flourishing and of peace. And it is because the true worship of God de-centres ourselves, that by it we are de-throned, delivered from our self-serving cycles of living an idolatrous vision of the world that the true worship of God fulfils us and is where we find our true home – that way of being at home with God.

It's the home of sharing in the life of the Trinity and refusing to engage in a power struggle with God over who should rule my life. We are fulfilled, made ourselves through worship precisely because we are not seeking to fill ourselves up but to give ourselves away. For there is no point in which we are closer to our fullness, in which we are more like God, than when our lives become offerings of self-gift.

Questions for further reflection

- What typically first comes to mind when you hear the word 'worship'? Has this chapter changed, helped or frustrated that thought at all?
- How has gathered worship in the church community affected your whole life as worship of God beyond the gathering? How have you seen this in others?
- Examine your life, even this particular day: where in your encounters with others do you see an encounter with God in worship – either in your own offering or another's in encountering you? What about your interactions with others reflects more of a sense of trying to de-throne God and elevate yourself or something else in worship?

Bibliography

Andrew McGowan, 2014, *Ancient Christian Worship: Early Christian Practices in Social, Historical, and Theological Perspective*, Grand Rapids, MI: Baker Academic.
Richard Rohr, 2011, *Falling Upward: A Spirituality for the Two Halves of Life*, San Francisco: Jossey-Bass.
James K. A. Smith, 2009, *Desiring the Kingdom: Worship, Worldview, and Cultural Formation*, Grand Rapids, MI: Baker Academic.
William Temple, [1939] 1985, *Readings in St John's Gospel*, New York: Morehouse.
Rowan Williams, 2014, 'Worship Makes our Lives Bigger and Better', *Catholic Herald* 27 September.

Further reading

Paul F. Bradshaw, 2010, *Early Christian Worship: A Basic Introduction to Ideas and Practice*, London: SPCK.

Andrew McGowan, 2014, *Ancient Christian Worship: Early Christian Practices in Social, Historical, and Theological Perspective*, Grand Rapids, MI: Baker Academic.

James K. A. Smith, 2009, *Desiring the Kingdom: Worship, Worldview, and Cultural Formation*, Grand Rapids, MI: Baker Academic.

3

Love in Listening:
An Invitation to Scripture

JARRED MERCER

Scripture: 'The Word of the Lord'

In most Christian churches, there is a strange ritual at the end
of a biblical reading when the reader says: 'The word of the
Lord', and the congregation receives it with thanksgiving,
responding: 'Thanks be to God'. What a remarkable assertion
– to read a bit of old text in front of a group of people and
claim to be speaking 'The word of the Lord'. Yet Christians
have always claimed that Scripture is in some sense God's
word to us. It shows us who God is, what God is like and who
we are in relation to God.

It's important to think about what we mean by this. Scripture
is not the word of God because it was miraculously written by
God's 'hand' or magically appeared from heaven. It is a human
book as much as it is 'the word of the Lord', and it was written,
collected and accepted as authoritative by a community of
people. Scripture grew out of a living, worshipping community
of faith. In other words, it isn't that the Church was born out
of Scripture (at least as Scripture includes the New Testament,
written after the community was formed), but that Scripture
was born from the community. This makes Scripture part of
living Christian tradition, part of what makes the Church the
Church, but also something made *by* the Church. This can also
be said of Hebrew Scripture, or the Old Testament, as it too

was born out of the living community of faith existing long before the experiences of the community were written down. That word 'tradition' does not simply mean 'what we've always done'. It is the truth and practice of our faith handed down to us, something that if it were lost, we would lose part of our identity. Scripture is part of that tradition, part of the 'deposit of faith' (cf. 1 Tim. 6.20; 2 Tim. 1.14) passed down, a foundation upon which we're built.

This isn't the whole story. But it is an important corrective to imagining that the Bible appeared as if from nowhere and then people read it and became Christians. Christians existed for decades before the New Testament books were written, and a few centuries before the final form of the New Testament was fully received as the authoritative 'word of the Lord' (what we call the 'canon'). There is a complicated history here. But for our purposes, this helps us to understand what we mean when we say Scripture is the word of God, what we mean by biblical authority and inspiration, and how we are to read, hear and interpret the Bible within the living community through which we receive and proclaim it.

To say the Bible is part of the tradition of the Church, that it was born out of the community rather than the other way round, is to say that it exists within the life of the Church alongside and with other essential aspects of our faith. It is, however, not *just* alongside other things. Scripture has always held a prime place in Christians' understanding of who they are and what they believe – a place of authority over the direction of that belief and identity. So, Scripture is something born from the people, but it also continually regenerates the people. It continues to reveal who this community is, how it lives and believes, and where it comes from. Scripture has always held a special place of authority for Christians, a place that even claims the divine voice. It's the part of what is handed down to us that illuminates the rest of what is handed down. The question is, how?

Christ: the heart of Scripture

Scripture is not the word of God because God dictated particular words through passive human agents. Scripture is part of the human struggle to know and love God, and part of how God meets us in our own human ways of knowing and understanding. And ultimately, it is the word of God because it is the witness to 'God the Word', Jesus Christ: the one who reveals to us, communicates to us what God is like. Scripture is God's word because it is continually pointing us to the one who is God's Word, God among us, God *translated* into human life and understanding.

From the earliest Christian interpreters (including within the New Testament), the Church has read the Bible as a book about Jesus Christ. Luke's Gospel tells us that Jesus interpreted Scripture, meaning the Hebrew Bible, as concerning himself (Luke 24.27). So, for Christians, the Bible as a whole is about Christ. It has many stories, it talks about many things, it contains various types of literature, but at the end of the day, it's all telling an overarching narrative of the salvation of the world through Christ. Jesus is the interpretive key to the whole biblical text. To read the Bible as a follower of Jesus and be able to say, 'This is the word of the Lord', is to read the Bible as continually bringing us to God in and through Christ.

In the incarnation, when God enters our human life in Christ, God shares with us who God is in a way that makes sense to us, that corresponds to our way of knowing and understanding. This is what we mean by revelation. We can access some knowledge of the unknowable, the infinite, the one who is forever and always beyond our grasp, not because we have God figured out, but because this unsearchable infinite one has come among us saying, 'this is who I am'. We can never have God-like knowledge of God, we only know from within the confines of our humanity, so God lovingly communicates to us within those restrictions in the person of Jesus Christ, who is the boundless love of God living within the boundaries of human life (see Mercer, pp. 51–62).

Scripture is not a collection of stories or a list of rules. It isn't an instruction manual or 'road map' for life. With Scripture we find ourselves in a world in which God has made a home with us. Because God has come among us, Scripture as God's story becomes *our* story too. The Bible, in other words, is an invitation. It's an invitation to meet God the Word, Jesus Christ, and be brought into God's embrace in the power of the Holy Spirit.

Holy Spirit: the inspiration of Scripture

This invitation to God's Word and God's embrace points us to what we mean by 'inspiration'. 2 Timothy 3.16 says all Scripture is 'inspired by God', or 'God-breathed'. This isn't to say that God dictated particular words, but that God moves through Scripture. This means that the Holy Spirit guided biblical authors but didn't then cease investing in Scripture or using it graciously for our progress in faith. Scripture is used by the Holy Spirit to bring us into relationship with Jesus and one another. Because that is the whole point. Scripture is never trying to lead us to Scripture. Scripture's purpose is to lead us to God. It's God's word because it moves us towards God the Word.

The inspiration of the Holy Spirit means that the Spirit is using the words of human writers to provide us with the truth, to open us up to God's grace, and to draw us into God's very life, so that we find ourselves wrapped up in the story of our redemption that meets us in Scripture. And Scripture's purpose of deepening relationships between God and humanity unfolds throughout the Bible. The Bible's whole story is the story of God's love for humanity and humanity's response to God's love. The issue is that human response is often failure, and even when faithful, it's never a perfect return of God's love. That is, until Jesus.

Jesus is the key to reading Scripture because he inhabits perfectly that relationship of receiving God's love and responding in perfect love to God. Scripture is working all along to reveal who God is and who we are – God's love towards us and what it means to live in response to God's love. Jesus shows us this, enacts this, fulfils this, perfectly. The inspiration of the Spirit in Scripture is the work of drawing us into that relationship with God that Jesus shares – one of union with God the Word. We discover ourselves involved in the human struggle to know God and make God known that we see in the text so that the movement of our own lives shares in Christ's response of love. The Spirit's 'breathing' through the text is not a divine over-taking – not a removal of the text from being human, but a uniting of the whole story of God's loving pursuit of the world in the person of Jesus Christ and a drawing of us into that story through invitation and embrace – stirring us up as Christ's body, to hear, interpret and respond.

No contest: the authority of Scripture

Some have argued that the inspiration of the Holy Spirit in Scripture is a 'verbal' inspiration, meaning that the Holy Spirit dictated word for word what we have as our Bible. On this view the words are not inspired in their movement into and through the community of readers as they live them but on the page in their original script. Inspiration is a 'then' rather than a 'then and now' reality. The danger here is Scripture becoming a historical fact book, a chronicle of events, or a textbook to teach us doctrines about God and the world, rather than an instrument of God's revelation through which God encounters us *now* and moves us beyond the text into relationship with the one to whom the text continually points.

Christians have generally not made this identification of the words of the Bible with the Word of God but taught that it opened the faithful hearer up to the Word of God, who is, according to Scripture itself, Jesus Christ (see John 1.1–18). The view of the Bible as the word of God *contained* sees that word not so much to be interpreted and brought into conversation with the lives of people as it does the word written down and preserved.

This at points places Scripture at odds with other forms of knowledge, as the Bible becomes an apologetic argument, a 'theory' among other competing 'theories' about God and the world. It's a type of biblical authority that is authoritarian: if truths we learn by other means are not exactly as described as an event in the Bible, then the Bible must 'conquer' that knowledge and prove it untrue. But Scripture doesn't stand over and against 'competing' accounts of the world. Scripture isn't involved in a contest for truth or reality. It *is* reality as we know it. Scripture is what is *most real* about the world. Liberation through Christ, the salvation of the world, the narrative of God's action in and with us, is simply the reality of the world and of us and of everything, meaning it includes so-called 'conflicting' accounts and truth wherever we find it ('all truth is God's truth' as goes the common paraphrase of St Augustine).

Reading Scripture in competition with what we know to be true by other means of reason, science or history is due to misunderstandings about the nature of Scripture. It's expecting Scripture to be something it isn't. And this competitive view forces us to make decisions between two truths – truth about God and our relationship to God in Scripture, and truth about the world we live in and ourselves living within it learned elsewhere.

But, if we do not believe that the purpose of the Bible is to give clear, factual and material knowledge of every subject it mentions and instead is to reveal the truth of who God is and what our relationship to God and one another should be, we can read the text as drawing us into the narrative of God's loving redemption of the world. We can know that a factual blunder about when Quirinius was the legate in Syria in Luke's Gospel (Luke 2.2), or the details of a battle in the Book of Joshua do not affect the truth of the text and its movement that we're drawn into for our salvation.

The real significance of misjudgements about Scripture's character is that they affect the way we read Scripture. If you think the Bible is primarily law, your view of God and others is going to be primarily concerned with right moral behaviour. The aim of relationships will become moral influence, setting oneself apart from lawbreakers, and perhaps even fear, seeing every difference from your way of life as attack, or persecution, or changing values that reflect what you see as given directly from the Bible. If you treat the whole Bible as proverbial wisdom, then you may not care if any of it is actually historical. Scripture will be no more than a spiritual guide divorced from real everyday life (an impossible scenario for those who confess belief in the incarnation).

Some of this is as simple as recognizing that the Bible is a very diverse book – or set of books, actually. It's been said that as soon as you think you have the Bible figured out you turn the page and it turns into something else (Williams, p. 25)! There are various genres of literature coming from various perspectives, and different authors who lived in very different times and contexts. The Bible contains history and songs, proverbs and wisdom literature, poetry and so much more. So, if you read an ancient Hebrew poem about the nature of the world as God's creation and God's relationship to that creation and assume it is not a poem but a historical account of how the universe was formed, you come across a difficult dilemma. If you imagine that what we read in the Bible and what we know from scientific accounts are in competition with one another, you will have to choose *either* the Bible *or* reason. But if we stop pretending Scripture is what it isn't, we can meet God through and within it and also not be at odds with what we know clearly to be true about the world or ignore the beauty of what we can learn through other means. Scripture does not stand up to scientific scrutiny in the way a virus, or a fossil, or a star does, not because it's deficient or untrue, but because it has never, ever attempted to do so. We shouldn't try to force it to or expect it to start.

An understanding of Scripture that puts it at odds with reason (often called biblicism, fundamentalism, or sometimes biblical inerrancy) not only affects how we read Scripture, it also claims that Scripture retains its authority in and of itself. The Bible takes the authoritative position that only God should fill, as it becomes synonymous with the Word of God (i.e. God the Word), leading Scripture's authority into the realm of authoritarianism. But, as N. T. Wright points out:

> When John declares that 'in the beginning was the word', he does not reach a climax with 'and the word was written down' but 'and the word became flesh'. The authority of Scripture, a critically important concept in Christianity, only makes sense as a way of speaking about 'the authority of the triune God, exercised somehow *through* scripture. (Wright, p. 17)

This brings us again to the inspiration of Scripture as God's movement through it and towards and in us: renewing us, converting us, and inviting us to continue that movement of God's love towards and in others.

Moving towards God: scriptural authority in prayer and worship

Communication is a two-way street. We meet God among us in Scripture because Scripture continually points us to Christ. And Christ, as God with us in our humanity, is God coming to us while bringing us towards God. In uniting God and humanity God the Word does not only communicate God to us, but is human life 'communicated to', expressed, brought into union with divine life. And this two-way movement is part of our reading of Scripture as well. Scripture opens us up to God's revelation to us – it is a divine linguistics, but it also gives a grammar for how to speak to God. It's a framework and authority for our life of prayer.

This makes reading Scripture central in our worship, preaching and the prayers passed down through the centuries. The entirety of the Church's liturgy and worship is shaped by

Scripture – both in form and content. Almost everything we say in our liturgies is taken directly from Scripture. We pray the Psalms, read from the whole biblical text, hear it proclaimed and even take our form of worship from the witness of early Christians in Scripture (principally in the Eucharist). Those in traditions or denominations whose worship is not centred on liturgy and isn't shaped around the prayers of Scripture and a lectionary covering the whole Bible will need to address how Scripture is authoritative for their worship and prayer. They have to ask: 'How is Scripture guiding us towards God, rather than existing as a one-way street of "God towards us" in revelation?'

There is a great risk that without liturgy and lectionary, the 'authority' of Scripture is more defined by what the preacher demands the Bible says, or what the denominational or cultural positions are regarding what the Bible teaches, than the words themselves. (This can, of course, happen in churches with set liturgies and lectionaries as well!) Certain human behaviours, political beliefs or forms of relationships are declared to be 'biblical' and others are not, as particular parts of the Bible are excised and 'applied' to life, rather than the whole of Scripture *being* our life. And it's easy to see how the authority of the Bible can turn into the authoritarianism of the Bible teacher. This also affects Scripture's purpose to change us, convict us, and bring about conversion. If we use Scripture to continually affirm ourselves in how we already think and live, transformation of individual's lives and change in the community become less possible, or even desirable.

When Scripture is genuinely authoritative in our worship, not only guiding principles or beliefs, but actively drawing us into God's presence in prayer and devotion, it renews and transforms us, converting us towards the love and mercy of Christ.

Performative reading: participation with Scripture

Anyone can read the Bible like any other book – full of mystery, excitement, confusing paradoxes, outlandish stories. It can be read as a classic of literature that has influenced successive literature arguably more than any other text. But the Bible becomes *Scripture* when we encounter Christ, the Word of God, by the Spirit working through it and in us. That encounter, and the resulting renewal and transformation it brings, points out the performative nature of scriptural interpretation. We read, hear and interpret Scripture as a community in worship, prayer and devotion, we meet Christ among us through Scripture, and in turn our reading becomes much more than reading, it becomes an act of love.

Entering into the story, making sense of ourselves and our world in that overarching narrative of Christ's redemption, is the text reading us – scrubbing out barely legible, half-hearted, expressions of our humanity that we walk in daily and bending the 'words' of our own life – what our living 'communicates' – into a clear message of hope. It's a reading that humanizes us, drawing us into that fullness of our humanity seen in Jesus.

Often the idea of living out the text of Scripture is thought of in terms of 'application': finding certain actions or ways of thinking that we can take from the text and apply in our lives. There are certainly things directly applicable to life in Scripture, but to live harmoniously with the story is not looking for lessons or moral undertones – locating ways of living that are 'biblical'. There are not 'biblical' things and other non-'biblical' things, the 'biblical' is the self-giving love of Jesus Christ, and that love lived out among us still. It is *us* walking into the invitation set before us in the story of our salvation.

This is about participation in the life of Jesus, becoming the Body of Christ that Scripture leads us towards all along (which is why its primary place of reading has always been in the Eucharist). And this is the life of love. It's a continual de-centring of ourselves – not constantly affirming ourselves, not the authoritarian view of biblical interpretation that weighs in heavy and makes sure our way of living or thinking is congratulated. But quite the opposite. Faithful reading is opening ourselves up to the piercing of the Spirit, humbly acknowledging our need of change and recognizing how much we don't know. Faithful reading rips us from the centre of our own lives, making room for others – turning us outward in the sacrificial, undying love we meet in Christ. As St Augustine was so keen to point out: 'Anyone who thinks that he has understood the divine scriptures or any part of them, but cannot by his understanding build up this double love of God and neighbour, has not yet succeeded in understanding them' (*De doctrina*, 1.36.41).

'Thanks be to God'? Reading difficult texts

If reading Scripture is leaning into God's love, entering the story of Christ, what about texts that appear to move contrary to love? If we look to Jesus to learn who God is, we see a God who is poured out in self-giving love – who *is* love. But many parts of Scripture present God as vengeful, haughty, violent even. How are we to stand up and read stories of God's people rejoicing in gratuitous violence, genocide and hatred and proclaim: 'The word of the Lord', or even more, respond in gratitude: 'Thanks be to God'?

It can be tempting just to leave those parts out (and if you aren't using the lectionary, it's easy to do!). But the first thing to realize is that just because something is recorded in Scripture, it doesn't mean God condones it, or that people who believed they were doing the will of God were actually right about that. If Jesus is the interpretive key to understanding Scripture, when people report that God is rage-filled and hungry for blood and claim their destructive actions are at the behest of God, we can be quite sure they've got it wrong. Scripture itself makes this evident. Jesus turns much of what people thought about God completely on its head. On the issue of vengeance, for example: 'You have heard that it was said, "An eye for an eye and a tooth for a tooth." But I say to you, Do not resist an evildoer. But if anyone strikes you on the right cheek, turn the other also' (Matt. 5.38–39). When we understand the inspiration and authority of Scripture not as God dictating words that people record but the Spirit moving through authors and readers, drawing them to God, we begin to see the Spirit bringing the whole of creation and all human living – *all of it* – into God's love.

Jesus' own reading of Scripture emphasizes this. When Jesus comes to the point of death, he cries out words of Psalm 22: 'My God, my God, why have you forsaken me?' (Matt. 27.46; Mark 15.34). He quotes other biblical texts throughout his life from the whole range of human emotions and experiences, the whole of our relationship to God – forsakenness and abandonment, faith and doubt, hope and despair. And the whole of the human condition – the beautiful and the despicable, the hopeless and the triumphant, is offered up and brought home to God. Jesus doesn't come before God offering up only the presentable parts of us, or the digestible and pleasing aspects of creation. He brings all of it, he redeems all of it, he carries all of it through the cross and into resurrection life. Scripture, as the word that discloses the Word, does the same thing. It brings every aspect of who we are, our mistakes and failures, our loves and joys, our sorrows and grief, the times when we have been faithful and when we've got it horribly wrong, into communion with God, and, in Christ, brings God into all the muck and mire of our fragile human life.

The Bible can be a difficult book. Sometimes obscure, sometimes vividly grotesque, but that is because that's how our lives are. This is what it means for human persons to be travelling through, hobbling through, stumbling through this story of redemption. The inclusion of overwhelming and difficult aspects of the biblical story is the inclusion of the aspects of our lives we find overwhelming and difficult, maybe even impossible, in God's embrace.

And that renewal is key. All this is leading towards Scripture's own focus and purpose: invitation – to draw us into that embrace, to bring us to *conversion*.

Conversion: the invitation of Scripture

Reading Scripture is discovering that God's story is our story, too. And following this invitation into God's story is not simply plucking out general principles that can be applied to life or following examples of what we see in the text. In fact, we will come across parts of Scripture that seem not to relate or apply at all to our lives. But we can follow the movement of the text, the 'way the words run', as it's been so aptly put: not necessarily by asking, 'what precise application to my particular situation, or direct command or instruction am I being asked to follow?', but, 'what kind of life is the text calling me to? What is the text asking of me, or pointing out in me? What conversion is needed in my life right now? How is the text of Scripture "reading" me as I read it?'

This call to conversion is not the same each time we confront the text or are 'read' by it. We read and hear and re-read and listen again not because we may have missed something last time, or we've forgotten things and need to be reminded, but because each time we can be converted anew. Each reading calls us to a new response because the text is not static or passive, but 'living and active' (Heb. 4.12). And the real wonder of this, the awe-inspiring beauty of it, is that if God's Spirit really is present with us, moving through the text, working in our own lives, and inviting us to respond, if this really is 'our story', then we all still have a part to play.

Questions for further reflection

- Communication is a two-way street. How might a practice of praying Scripture, rather than simply reading it, change your approach to the Bible? As you pray along with Scripture, what is the invitation you're receiving? What conversion or need for change is confronting you?

- What parts of Scripture do you find most difficult? What might these texts be revealing to you about God and yourself? How might they be inviting you to conversion and change?

Bibliography

Augustine of Hippo, *De doctrina christiana*, R. P. H. Green (trans.), 1997, *On Christian Teaching*, Oxford: Oxford University Press.

Jarred Mercer, 2019, 'Love Personified – The Incarnation', in Jennifer Strawbridge, Jarred Mercer and Peter Groves, *Love Makes No Sense: An Invitation to Christian Theology*, London: SCM Press, pp. 51–62.

N. T. Wright, 2005, *Scripture and the Authority of God*, London: SPCK, 17. Referenced in William Lamb, 2013, *Scripture: A Guide for the Perplexed*, London: Bloomsbury, p. 159.

Rowan Williams, 2014, *Being Christian*, London: SPCK.

Further reading

John Barton, 2010, *The Bible: The Basics*, Abingdon: Routledge.

William Lamb, 2013, *Scripture: A Guide for the Perplexed*, London: Bloomsbury.

Jennifer Strawbridge, 2019, 'Love Outspoken – Scripture and the Church', in *Love Makes No Sense*, pp. 119–28.

Rowan Williams, 2014, *Being Christian*, London: SPCK, pp. 21–40.

4

Love Incarnate:
An Invitation to the Sacraments

PETER GROVES

Signs and symbols

At the seminary in Cambridge where I trained for ordained
ministry, there was a corridor which ended in the entrance
to a large lecture room. On the door to that entrance was a
sign reading 'Please keep this door closed at all times'. As a
philosopher friend of mine took delight in pointing out, there
didn't seem to be much point in a door which was kept closed
at all times. How would one ever enter the room? It is true that
my friend enjoyed pedantry (he once answered the question "Is
this lift going up or down?" with the word "Yes"!) but I had
to agree that that sign was not the most effective of notices. It
did issue an instruction (disguised as a petition), but it was an
instruction that was impossible to obey without removing the
very purpose of the door to which it was fixed.

Signs point to things, they convey information or indicate
a course of action. A good sign is an effective sign, it tells me
something helpful, or enables me to do what I want to do or
reach my intended destination. A bad sign will be difficult to
read or hard to understand. Signs are closely related to symbols, things which stand for other things or ideas, perhaps in
visual communication or in the telling of stories. In William
Golding's novel *Lord of the Flies* a group of boys, escaping a
nuclear explosion, attempt to create their own society on the

island where they have landed. In their fledgling democracy, a large shell – the conch – serves to represent order and government: it is used as a trumpet to summon the boys together, and it is held in the hand of the person speaking to ensure each has a free and fair voice at meetings. As events descend into chaos and violence, so the conch loses its symbolic authority over the boys, a development which only increases its symbolic power within the story: the conch is smashed at the same time as the boy called Piggy, the system's great defender, is murdered.

We tend to associate signs with something specific, while symbolic meaning is often deeper and further reaching, but there is no neat distinction here: symbolic objects and actions are often also signs of something particular. Harry Potter's scar is a sign of the attack made upon him when a baby by Voldemort, but also a symbol of the struggle and conflict with evil which will be his story. At the beginning of William Thackeray's *Vanity Fair*, the remarkable heroine Rebecca Sharp is gifted a copy of Dr Johnson's *Dictionary* as she leaves school. No sooner is the carriage under way than Becky dismissively flings the volume to the ground. Her action shows us her contempt for the establishment from which she has graduated, but points also to a wider disdain for form and convention which will be the pattern of her life and of the narrative which she dominates.

Long before the English novel was thought of, the Jewish and Christian scriptures were filled with actions and events which point beyond their particular context to a wider truth, a truth about God and humanity. The Lord's rescuing of the people of Israel from slavery in Egypt by commanding the powers of nature is much more than an individual decision to liberate that particular set of people. It is a sign that the God of Israel is the creator and that comparison with other 'gods' can only be nonsensical, as the prophet called Second Isaiah (Isa. 40–55) is so keen to observe. When the fingers of a hand appear and write on the wall in the fifth chapter of the book of Daniel, they are both a sign that King Belshazzar is about to meet his fate, and a sign of the broader truth that human beings will be judged by the God who created them. In

all four Gospels (though at different points in the narrative)
Jesus upends the tables of the money changers in the temple
precincts to bring an end to particular financial abuse, but also
to symbolize the revolution which he inaugurates as the herald
of God's kingdom. In the Gospel of John, the works of power
which Jesus performs are specifically called signs, drawing the
reader's attention to the fact that the abundance of new wine
at the marriage at Cana, or the healing of the official's son, are
seen to point beyond their contexts to the universal truth of
Jesus' unique status and authority.

Divine and human

Christianity expresses that status and authority in its teaching
that Jesus Christ is both divine and human, the doctrine we
call the incarnation (from the Latin *incarnere*, to be 'enfleshed',
referencing God entering human life in Christ). And from that
central Christian belief flows all that Christians have to say
about the signs of God's love which they call sacraments. The
English word 'sacrament' arises from the Latin word for an
oath, and, as signs of something sacred or holy, the Christian
sacraments are pledges of God's love for and relationship with
the world which God creates and sustains. We use the word
holy to describe that which is set apart for the purposes of
God, and the peculiar function of the sacraments in the life of
the church is both the celebration and the effect of that setting
apart: in the sacraments, God points us to the truth of God's
love, and also brings that love into new ways of being, by
bringing about particular things in the created world through
the people and objects which make up that world of God's
creation.

According to theological jargon, a sacrament is a sign which
'effects that which it signifies'. To say this is to say that a sacrament is both a sign and more than a sign. An arrow might
point me in a particular direction, indicating the place to which
I wish to go. If it does so accurately, it will achieve the purpose

for which it was intended – helping me find my way to my destination. But it will not achieve my goal for me, it will not physically transport me to the end of my journey. I will do that myself, perhaps with the aid of something mechanical such as a car or a bike. The sign has pointed the way, but I have had to put the miles in. A Christian sacrament, however, brings about that to which it points. So in the celebration of the Eucharist, I am not simply shown an image of communion with the life of God and God's people, I am actually ushered into that communion by the sacrament of the body and blood of Christ. Those present at a baptism see the symbols of new life which signify union with Christ in his death and resurrection, but the person being baptized is actually born anew, given a life transformed and recreated, as they are enfolded into the life of God the Son.

To say more about what this means, we need to return to the centrality of the incarnation. At the heart of Christian theology is the person of Jesus, the human being who is God. Everything about Jesus of Nazareth demonstrates to the world the reality of the divine life. The things Jesus says and does point us towards the truth about God, they are, in that sense, signs of something above and beyond their individual occurrence. As with any effective sign, the words and actions of Jesus aid us in our search for the truth about God. But they do a great deal more than that, because Jesus of Nazareth is more than a particular human being who lived in a particular place at a particular time. The insistence of incarnational theology is that Jesus of Nazareth is also God, that everything I can say about the person I call Jesus I can also, paradoxically, say about God in the mystery of the incarnation. Jesus is both a sign of the divine, and divinity itself, pointing us towards the real thing which is no different from the one doing the pointing.

So sacraments can be sacraments because the reality of Jesus Christ – a sign and much more than a sign – underlies all Christian talk of signification. And there is another essential sense in which sacraments are incarnational, in that sacraments are something physical. In Christian theology sacraments are not simply ideas or abstract concepts, they are actions in the world undertaken by and through the physical reality which is God's good creation. Here we are at the heart of the Christian claim: that God, incarnate in Jesus Christ, does not transform the world from a distance but identifies with it. God becomes a part of the very thing which God has made, and which is sustained for every moment of its existence by the outpouring of God's love. When we call Jesus by the name 'Emmanuel', God with us, we are both embracing the essence of Christian theology and dismissing the all too prevalent notion that God is something or someone distant, far off, detached or remote from the lives and loves and hopes and fears of the world God has made. There are few more disastrous lines in popular hymnody than the request, in the carol 'Away in a manger', that the Lord Jesus should 'look down from the sky'. The whole of the Christmas story is a rejection of such a picture. God is not in the sky; God is among us in Jesus Christ.

The physical world

The incarnation reminds us that, far from something abstract or immaterial, Christianity is a physical faith. Christian teaching about God is also teaching about matter, and the part matter or stuff has to play in the story of God's relationship with the world. The stuff which is the body of Jesus is essential to that story, but it is a story which involves not just the stuff which is Jesus but nothing less than all the stuff there is, everything which is part of the totality we call creation. That story tells of the God who is material, the God who becomes stuff like you and me out of love for all that God has made. In the incarnation, God becomes part of God's own making to unite it with God's own self.

So the sacraments, as physical signs of the reality of God's love, are rooted in the truth of God incarnate. In turn, that truth cannot be separated from the Christian doctrine of creation. Talk of creation is not talk of a God who starts things off, or a watchmaker who designs a working mechanism and lets it go. To know God as creator is to know that everything which exists depends for every moment of its existence on the God who creates and sustains it. What it means to exist, to be, is to be held in being by the love of God. The very first chapter of the Bible reminds us over and again that God saw what God had made, and it was good. The incarnation is not an addition to creation so much as the end or goal of all God's making. The glorification of matter in the person of Jesus is the source for the transformation of all created things. The signs we call sacraments are themselves particular affirmations of the goodness of creation, brought to fulfilment in the person of Jesus.

In recent times, theologians have spent much ink and energy discussing the best ways in which to talk about God in relation to the world, and the best ways to talk about the world from a theological perspective. Many in the twentieth century were rightly suspicious of attempts to categorize the divine as if God could be considered and described the way one would describe an object, or a part of the universe. The desire to avoid such a distortion has sometimes led theologians to spring back too far the other way, setting the idea of God over against the idea of the world, separating these two areas of discussion entirely. But there is then a danger of enabling the notion of the 'secular', the idea that there is a world of people, events, concepts and ideas which ought to be thought of without any recourse to God at all. Instead, if we believe in the God who created all things out of nothing, it really does not make sense to exclude theological ways of speaking from any area of human existence. The incarnation crystallizes this truth, prohibiting Christian theology from descending into pure abstraction. To talk of God is, for Christians, to talk of Jesus Christ, and the particularity of the incarnation is lived out in the Church through the sacramental life.

What does this sacramental life mean? Theologically, it means that the signs we call sacraments are the working out of that which is already true about the love of God in creation and redemption. The love of God is poured out into everything which is made and personified in the incarnation of the Son. God's act of becoming human is the supreme act of divine self-emptying, as Paul puts it in the second chapter of Philippians. But this self-emptying is not a new decision so much as an expression of what is always and eternally true about God, in the dynamic self-giving which we call the life of the Trinity: Father, Son and Holy Spirit. The practical outworking of that self-giving love in the lives of human beings we call grace – the free gift of God which enables us to be more than we can be if left to ourselves. Sacraments are vehicles of grace, that is to say they are particular ways in which God chooses to effect the reality of divine love in the ordinary day to day life of the ordinary physical world.

That word 'ordinary' is important, because the Christian sacraments are a pledge to God's people that the love of Christ is never absent. Sacraments are worldly things – physical signs and actions – which are also heavenly things: means by which God unites God's life with the lives of people. Sacraments represent, therefore, a refusal to accept that anything is truly 'secular', removed or separate from the presence of God in the world. And the central truth that God shows up in the ordinariness of human existence then becomes the basis for the sacramental life which Christians are called to live.

Gift, offering and service

What does this living look like? First of all, sacramental life is a gift. The love of God which animates the Christian life is the free gift of God freely received in the grace of baptism and through the presence of God's animating Spirit in every moment of our existence. To live as a Christian is always first to acknowledge that one's life is not one's own but is given in trust for God's good purpose (remember that 'sacramentum' originally meant 'oath'). The response that gift enables is made by the proper ordering of our lives in relation to God – through prayer and worship, for example – by the Christian call to offering. What is received has been given for a purpose, and that purpose is to offer life to others. The incarnational mission of Jesus is then carried out in the life of the church through those who are the celebrants and hence recipients of Christ's sacramental grace. And 'celebrants' here does not refer to those who are in holy orders, it refers to the whole people of God.

The pattern of offering we seek is found, as we have seen, in Jesus, and so the offering the Christian is called to make is always one of service. The Son of Man came not to be served, but to serve, says Jesus (Mark 10.45). The one who is the Lord of all takes the towel and the bowl and washes the feet of those he calls his friends. The humility of God in Christ is not an act to grab our attention, it is the reality of divine love lived out in a human life. The sacraments demonstrate and enact that incarnational love which is the free gift of God, offered to God's people, that they might offer themselves in service to the world around them. As incarnational actions, the sacraments show us human beings in their right relationship with God – the relationship of loving participation in the divine life – and also effect that right relationship by enabling human beings to live lives of love and service to one another. The sacraments point to the love of Christ and they bring about the love of Christ, and they do this because they are the vehicles of Christ's own loving presence in the world he has redeemed.

As we have emphasized, there is something specific about sacraments. They are particular actions in particular contexts and they are celebrated and lived out by particular people. Over the centuries, Christians have differed over which specific actions of the church are rightly called 'sacraments'. However, few Christians would quarrel with the contention that the most important of the acts we call sacramental are the two 'domin-ical sacraments' (sacraments 'of the Lord'): Baptism and the Eucharist. We see both actions featuring significantly in the Gospels, both straightforwardly (in the baptism of Christ and the Last Supper, for example) and symbolically (Jesus calls his death his 'baptism' in Mark 10, and invites those who believe in him to eat his flesh and blood in John 6). These two, the central actions of the Church, are each given a chapter to themselves elsewhere in this book.

The practicality of love

To look at the practical outworking of the sacramental life, then, we turn to some of the other things which Christians call 'sacramental'. Take, for example, reconciliation (the celebration of God's forgiveness through the individual confession of sins and the pronouncement of absolution). The terminology is important here. The sacrament of reconciliation is often called simply 'confession', but that word does not offer a full description. In this sacrament, two people come together as the Church (in Matthew 18.20, Jesus reminds us that he is present where two or three are gathered in his name) to give thanks for and enact the forgiveness which God offers to God's people in the person of Jesus Christ. This is not a simplistic contractual arrangement, in which a particular reward is the result of performing a particular action. Rather, it is the acknowledgement that the love of God permeates everything about our lives, and that everything which is true about ourselves, including the very many truths we would rather not admit, forms part of our relationship with God. As we have seen, the love of God which enfolds us in all our sin and weakness, is already always being poured out in the perfect offering of Christ to the Father, and so the forgiveness we receive in the particular act of the sacrament of reconciliation is no different from the love of Christ which already animates our lives. In the sacramental action, however, that same love works through specific contexts and people to bring about specific things in their lives.

Among the most important of those specific things is the openness to others which is the result of sacramental grace. The love of God effects change in human beings not in abstract, but by real things happening to real people. The recipient of grace is the one whose heart is enlarged by the gentle insistence of God's love, worming its way in beyond our fears and our insecurities. That enlargement in turn gives us a heart which is big enough to be open to the world and the relationships in which we belong. Receiving sacramental grace is always to be called to sacramental service.

To take another example, the sacraments of healing, which are so vital and yet so unnoticed aspects of Christian life, do not simply represent the need for the church to respond to Christ's example of healing. The particular act of anointing the sick with oil blessed for the purpose is always a sign of the wider Christian call to respond to those in need. In Christ we see the love of God incarnate demonstrated in the embrace and transformation of human disease and limitation. In the Gospels Christ calls his followers to tend to those who suffer. In the sacramental action of healing the Church is laying all human life, all created physicality, at the feet of the one who made it, the feet scarred and wounded by human abuse and hatred. The one who lives the Christian life lives out the sacramental call to healing by responding to sickness, by loving the one whose need is greater than our own, by extending into our day-to-day existence the particular grace of sacramental anointing, whether or not that specific action is one they have ever experienced.

Sacraments are about life. About the life of God first of all, and also and always about the life of those to whom God gives that gift of life. Sacraments are actions in which the goodness of creation is shown to the world, and by which the presence of the incarnate Christ is made manifest in the ordinariness of the world with which he identifies himself in love. The gift of God which is offered to us in the love of Christ is ours to receive and to offer in service to the world around us. That offering and that service will take individual and specific form in the individual and specific contexts of each of our lives. But the sacramental life which we are called to live will never belong to any of us alone. To be invited to share the joy of the sacraments is to be invited to live as one of the people of God, as a member of the Body of Christ throughout all times and ages.

No one is an island, as John Donne almost said, and though the sacraments are God's gift to individuals, there is nothing remotely individualistic about the Christian life.

Questions for further reflection

- The sacraments are called signs, but also called 'holy mysteries'. Is there a contradiction here?
- Medieval theologians debated whether grace was contained in the sacraments as water is in a vessel. Why was this an important question?
- How significant are Christian disagreements over how many sacraments there are?

Further reading

Andrew Davison, 2013, *Why Sacraments?*, London: SPCK.
John Macquarrie, 1997, *A Guide to the Sacraments*, London: SCM Press.
Peter Waddell, 2012, *Joy: the meaning of the Sacraments*, London: SCM Press.

5

Love in New Creation:
An Invitation to Baptism

JONATHAN JONG

The next time you walk into a church – especially an old church – keep a lookout for the baptismal font. They are essentially basins, elevated off the ground and often held in ornately carved stone or marble or wood. Unless the church has messed things about, you should find the font near the entrance, which is a way of saying that Christians enter and become part of the Church through baptism. Baptism is the Church's initiation ritual.

Baptisms are mostly rather tame affairs, as initiation rituals go. To baptize a baby, a priest holds her over the font filled with water, and with one hand scoops some of it up to pour onto her head: once, in the name of the Father; and again, in the name of the Son; and a third time, in the name of the Holy Spirit. She might cry a bit, but only because the splashes of water come as a bit of a shock. The experience is even less startling for adults, who are similarly thrice doused. If they shed any tears at all, it is for rather different, more emotionally sophisticated reasons.

Baptism did not always look like this. For example, the Gospels clearly say that Jesus was baptized by John the Baptist in the Jordan River, not indoors and over a sculptural basin. Medieval and Renaissance paintings of Jesus's baptism often depict him standing in the river, with John pouring water on his head, but most biblical scholars believe that Jesus would have been fully submerged. They point out that the Greek word *baptízō* implies dipping or plunging. There is also some evidence that early Christians preferred baptism by full immersion. Certainly, the late-first-century text called the *Didache* (Greek again, for 'teaching') treats our common practice of baptism by pouring as a last resort, acceptable but not ideal. Even after Christians stopped baptizing people in rivers, we built baptisteries outside of the main church buildings where even adults could be fully immersed. This was common long before we had the little fonts we find in churches nowadays.

Our current common practice has the virtue of being rather convenient, especially in its efficient use of space. But it is a pity that baptisms by immersion have become quite rare, except among Eastern Orthodox, Baptist and Pentecostal churches. It is a pity because immersion is a fitting symbol of the way that the New Testament makes theological sense of baptism. In the Gospels, baptism is linked to repentance: what John the Baptist offers is, according to Mark, 'a baptism of repentance for the forgiveness of sins' (1.4). There is an obvious resonance between this notion and the idea that baptism is a kind of cleansing: the water poured upon us washes away our sins, much as we might wash our hands under a tap.

There is, however, another strand of thought in the New Testament. In his letter to the Romans, St Paul writes that Christians have been 'buried with [Jesus] by baptism into death' (6.4). This idea is repeated in the letter to the Colossians (2.12). So, baptism is a cleansing, but it is also a kind of death: it is a participation in the death of Christ himself. It is easy to see how baptism by full immersion is an appropriate sign of this: in this act, a person is drowned, buried in a watery grave.

Baptism into death and new life

We do not usually tell parents that we are going to drown their babies in the waters of baptism, but perhaps we should. Perhaps we should say more about what the Christian life entails, to which our baptism calls us, and which it symbolizes in the form that it takes. To say that baptism is a death that brings new life implies that it is a most peculiar kind of death, and so it is. We are not plunged into the water to be abandoned there, but to emerge again, like Jesus coming up out of the Jordan at his baptism and out of the tomb on Easter morning.

The same passages in the New Testament that speak of us being baptized into Christ's death also tell us that this death is how we arrive at a new kind of life. That sentence from St Paul's letter to the Romans quoted above says in full: 'Therefore we have been buried with him by baptism into death, so that, just as Christ was raised from the dead by the glory of the Father, so we too might walk in newness of life' (6.4). Similarly in the letter to the Colossians, we are told that, having been buried with Christ in baptism, we are 'also raised with him through faith in the power of God, who raised him from the dead' (2.12).

Indeed, this theme of new life that requires death runs all throughout the New Testament. Jesus says that 'those who want to save their life will lose it, and those who lose their life for my sake, and for the sake of the gospel, will save it' (Mark 8.35; cf. Luke 9.24, 17.33; John 12.25), and again that 'If any want to become my followers, let them deny themselves and take up their cross and follow me' (Matt. 16.24; Mark 8.34; Luke 9.23). St Paul then asserts that 'it is no longer I who live, but it is Christ who lives in me. And the life I now live in the flesh I live by faith in the Son of God, who loved me and gave himself for me' (Gal. 2.20), and exhorts us to also consider ourselves 'dead to sin and alive to God in Christ Jesus' (Rom. 6.11).

Baptism and the freedom to love

What is this new life like then, that baptism brings? If baptism is a participation in Christ's death, then it must be a sacrificial death, undergone for the sake of others: and this indicates the kind of life Christians are called to lead, also for others' sake, which is to say a life of love. A life lived for others is, in some important ways, like being dead. Baptized into Christ's death and resurrection, we are in this new life, dead women and men walking, and therefore, free. Free, that is, from the egocentric insecurities that plague so many of us in life, the natural consequences of our cravings for wealth, esteem and power. Free also from the limitations of our natural tendencies, foisted upon us by biology and culture both, to prefer those who look and sound and worship like we do over those we consider inferior or perverse simply because they are different. In other words, baptism puts us to death in order to set us free for love.

The dead do not own property; nor can power benefit them. Even fame is pointless for them: what good does it do to the dead if their names continue to fall off the lips of the chattering classes? Our baptism tells the truth about us: neither do we need wealth and power and fame, which are irrelevant to our value, we who have died to the trappings of life as it has been sold to us by advertisers and politicians, and perhaps even by well-meaning parents and teachers who worry about us that we will be left behind if we are caught without beauty or erudition or influence or cold, hard cash. At some level, we all already know that our worth is not calculable in those terms, but still we chase them. The baptismal water splashes cold on our faces to wake us up to see that we are loved without condition and beyond compare by God who deigns to come and join us in the river as in the manger and on the cross and everywhere in between. We are free from needing to accumulate the sorts of things people always have everywhere, the gold and glory in whatever currency.

No wonder then, that Jesus tells the rich man to sell his possessions and give the money to the poor (Matt. 19.16–22; Mark 10.17–22; Luke 18.18–30). No wonder that Jesus calls those blessed who are derided, and woeful those who are esteemed (Matt. 5.3–12; Luke 6.20–23). The earliest Christian community, described in the Acts of the Apostles, seem to have known this well, who indeed 'were together and had all things in common; they would sell their possessions and goods and distribute the proceeds to all, as any had need' (2.44–45). That we find it difficult to imagine selling our possessions to share with others is as good a sign as any that we are not yet free from our material concerns, or at least that we do not yet believe that we have been set free.

The dead are free also from the allegiances owed by the living, such as to state and nation and even family. Baptism relativizes all our previous sources of identity, those group alignments from which we derive our comfort and self-esteem, often at the expense of those who are different from us. As St Paul observes: 'There is no longer Jew or Greek, there is no longer slave or free, there is no longer male and female; for all of you are one in Christ Jesus' (Gal. 3.28). These divisions give rise to sins most mundane and deadly: racism, sexism, xeno-phobia and other forms of prejudice and injustice that have, in the bloody course of history, manifested themselves in the atrocities of slavery, genocide and the systematic oppression of various minority groups. But these barriers of sex and race and citizenship, and even family, have been washed away by the baptismal waters.

Perhaps it seems odd to say that Christian faith frees us from our loyalties to state and family. After all, here in England, the Queen is the Supreme Governor of the Church of England: she nominates our bishops, and the Archbishop of Canterbury will eventually crown the new monarch, as his predecessors have done for centuries. Not since the reign of Theodosius I in the fourth century CE has there been the separation of church and state across Europe. Over the centuries since, many have died in battle for the sake of 'God, King and Country'. Even across the Atlantic, despite the First Amendment to the United States Constitution, Christianity – Protestantism in particular – has been cosy with political power for most of the country's history. Patriotism, not to say jingoism, seems to have become a Christian virtue.

Similarly, though perhaps more so in the United States than in the United Kingdom, Christianity is also closely associated with 'family values', which typically assumes an ideal of a heterosexual marital unit complete with biological offspring. A long litany of social changes in recent decades have been accused by some Christians of violating these values, including changes in attitudes towards gender roles, family planning and same-sex relationships. The privileging of the nuclear family is not unique to Christianity, of course. Even nonreligious people prioritize the needs and desires of their own parents and siblings, spouses and children over those of strangers, and certainly over those anonymous strangers who live and work far, far away.

In contrast to the historical and sociological facts as we find them, however, the Bible – and the New Testament in particular – is somewhat suspicious of both state and family. Even the Old Testament, which waxes messianic about King David, is at first critical of Israel's desire for a king at all (1 Sam. 8); in the centuries after that, many prophets indeed suffered at the hands of Israel and Judah's ruling classes. In the New Testament, the people of God have even more reason to dislike state power, living as they did under the rule of puppet vassals of the Roman Emperor. Matthew's Gospel accuses Herod the Great, the so-called king of the Jews, of trying to kill the baby Jesus by ordering the massacre of all male children in and around Bethlehem aged two years or under.

Herod's ersatz kingdom was then divided between four of his survivors, including Antipas who succeeded where his father had failed. Jesus suffered and died caught up in his political dance with Pontius Pilate, the Roman governor. The Herodian family ruled at the pleasure of Caesar, to whom Jesus famously said we should render the things that are his while rendering to God the things that are God's. Whatever it is that states may be said to own, Christians have always been clear that people – who bear the image of God who made us – are God's. This is truer still for those who are doubly God's, incorporated by baptism into Christ's own Body. We belong to no earthly power; none can claim our allegiance by right.

Our baptism is therefore a call to render ourselves unto

God, and not Caesar. For Christians, this has sometimes meant refusing to capitulate to the demands of the state, instead subjecting ourselves to its punitive power. From Jesus's refusal to answer Pilate's interrogation (John 19) to early Christians' refusal to fight in the Roman army to the civil disobedience of churches in their offering sanctuary to undocumented refugees and their marching for the rights of the disenfranchised and the welfare of workers, we are a people who have always known that our loyalty lies in a power and authority higher and more noble than anything to be found under a crown or an oath of political office.

If the New Testament's statements about state power are ambiguous, what it has to say about traditional family units is much less so. Jesus was, of course, conceived out of wedlock, and Joseph drops out of the narrative very early on. When his mother and brothers ask to speak to him, Jesus asks rhetorically 'Who are my mother and my brothers?' before declaring that 'Whoever does the will of God is my brother and sister and mother' (Mark 3.33, 35; cf. Matt. 12.46–50). He could be dismissive of others' filial obligations too, such as when one of his would-be followers asked to first let him bury his father: to this request, Jesus said, 'Let the dead bury their own dead' (Matt. 8.22; Luke 9.60). If that is too cryptic, Luke's Gospel also has Jesus saying: 'Whoever comes to me and does not hate father and mother, wife and children, brothers and sisters, yes, and even life itself, cannot be my disciple' (Luke 14.26). If Christianity has a positive doctrine of the family, it is first a doctrine of adoption, not of genetic ties. The Holy Family, recall, is not a biological phenomenon in the usual sense. And we are, after all 'children of God, who were born, not of blood or of the will of the flesh or of the will of man, but of God' (John 1.12–13).

None of this is to deny that there are passages of the Bible that exhort us to obey and honour state authorities (Rom. 13.1) and parents (Ex. 20.12; Eph. 6.2), and to be faithful spouses and kind parents (Prov. 5.18–20; Matt. 19.6; Col. 3.21). Some of them are admittedly reactionary, which just goes to show that biblical proof-texting is a fool's errand. Nor is the purpose of highlighting other parts of the Bible that cast a more critical eye on these venerable institutions to suggest that we ought never obey civil authorities and fulfil familial duties. Rather, it is to help us see that our baptism changes our relationships to these other elements of our identities. No earthly bonds can be absolute for us, and we are called to be vigilant against the idolatries of treating them so.

We are called, furthermore, to see beyond our tribes with eyes of love, and to work for the good of those we might consider strangers or even enemies. Indeed, the New Testament subverts both categories: in Christ, there are neither strangers nor enemies, only *neighbours*, that great gospel relation, of the oft-repeated 'You shall love your neighbour as yourself' (Lev. 19.18; Matt. 22.39; Mark 12.31; Rom. 13.9; Gal. 5.14; James 2.8), which in the parable of the Good Samaritan transcends differences ethnic and religious, enmities historic and current (Luke 10.25–37).

In other words, our baptism does not obliterate our particularities, but transforms them. We remain members of our tribes – our families and our ethnic groups, our political parties and nation-states – but in necessarily new ways. In John's Gospel, Jesus explains this new relationship by saying that we do not belong to the world, but are sent into it (17.16–18). Similarly, St Paul says that though he is free, belonging to no one, he has made himself a slave to all (1 Cor. 9.19–23).

Thus, our baptisms reorient us, so that we not only come from these families, nations and states but are called to them, called to love them not because they are in various ways like us but because they have been given to us to love. Even Jesus himself began by proclaiming the gospel to Jews, all within a hundred miles radius of his birthplace. And we are also called from them, and from the privileges they confer, to bear witness elsewhere, not only in Jerusalem but also 'in all Judea and Samaria, and to the ends of the earth' (Acts 1.8). Jesus too ended up, sometimes seemingly to his own surprise, ministering to Syrophoenicians (Matt. 15.21–28; Mark 7.24–30) and

Romans (Matt. 8.5–13; Luke 7.1–10); and the effects of his death and resurrection stretch further still. He may have said that salvation is from the Jews (John 4.22), but it is for the whole world.

Baptism, faith and hope

This may all sound either too good or too difficult to be true, this new kind of life, free from material and social insecurities, free to love beyond biological and cultural barriers, and to deny ourselves in order to offer ourselves for the sake of others. If so, then you are right. People complained about this sort of thing too in Jesus's own day, to which he replied, 'For mortals it is impossible, but for God all things are possible' (Matt. 19.26; Mark 10.27). Admittedly, this does not seem a very helpful observation; after all, we are the ones who are called to live this life, so it is not obvious what good it does us that God is omnipotent. The difficulty of Jesus's teaching and the apparent impossibility of the things he said did lead some of his disciples to abandon him. But when he asked the twelve, who would later be known as apostles, whether they too planned to leave, Simon Peter replied 'Lord, to whom can we go? You have the words of eternal life' (John 6.68).

It is not only Christianity that casts ideals too lofty to achieve, and yet too compelling to ignore. Consider the enterprise many people nowadays mistakenly consider the antithesis to religion, natural science. The goal of most scientists is truth: scientists are not, on the whole, satisfied with making accurate predictions or solving practical problems, though these too are gratifying accomplishments. It is not enough for them to be able to tell us when Halley's comet will next return (the year 2062, by the way): they want to know what they are made of and where they come from and why they move the way they do. It is not even enough for them to be able to cure us of our diseases: they want to know how bacteria evolved, how viruses reproduce, how cells mutate and turn malignant.

The history of science is, among other things, the history of ideas about how the world works, and there have been many such ideas, each old one falsified, overturned by new ones. Even now, scientists are pushing scientific theories to their limits, in the hope of breaking them to discover new ways of thinking about the world. They do not yet know what new theories lurk just beyond sight: all they know is that all old scientific theories have been false, and our current ones probably are too. They used to believe in phlogiston and aether and *élan vital*: and they now believe in quarks and dark energy and mirror neurons. Nobody knows if these hypothetical entities will ever be replaced, and if so, by what.

Indeed, nobody knows when or even whether scientists will ever arrive at a true picture of the hidden things in reality. This does not stop them from trying to get there, nor should it.

Or consider marriage, and the vows couples make to one another: the familiar vows are Christian, of course, but they are earnestly taken as ideals far beyond the Church. To have and to hold; for better for worse; for richer for poorer; in sickness and in health; to love and to cherish; till death. The evidence that any couple will live up to even the last promise alone is discouraging: in England and Wales, about a fifth of couples divorce by their tenth anniversary, and a third by their twentieth. (In other words, the common refrain that *half* of marriages end in divorce is false; but it's true that – according to the UK Office of National Statistics – around 40 per cent of couples married before 1995 have since divorced.) A cynic might dismiss marriage vows as naïve, but I would rather see them – like the scientist's commitment to pursuing truth – as a product of faith and hope, virtues hardly unfamiliar to Christians.

The Christian life – like marriage and science, and any life worth living – is an orientation towards the world that refuses the convenience of cynicism and dares instead to hope that we can, by the grace of God, love beyond our natural inclinations. And of course we will repeatedly fail to live up to these ideals. Every individual Christian life and the history of the Church is marked by conspicuous failures to live up to our baptisms.

We are called to live impossible lives. And while, for some, this leads to despair, it should not. There is nothing to fear from failure *per se*, only from the failure to then rise again. Resurrection is, after all, at the heart of Christian faith.

Baptism into the Body of Christ

There is another gift that comes together with our baptismal vocation, which has to do with something already mentioned at the very beginning of this chapter. Baptism is the initiation ritual of the Church: it is the way through which we enter the Church, and become part of it, the Body of Christ. We have, so far, focused on what this incorporation means for how we are called to live: to be Christ's Body is to be offered up as a living sacrifice, to participate here and now in Christ's work, accomplished once and for all on the cross. But, of course, to be Christ's Body is also to have God with us – Immanuel – as close to us as we are to our own bones and sinews, and closer. The New Testament repeats over and over again, even more than it does the command to love our neighbour, the conviction that we are *in Christ*, which is its way of expressing the incomparable nearness of God.

In the end, this is the point of baptism: union with Christ, and therefore with God. If baptism frees us from the bondages of insecurity and misaligned desires and mistaken identities, it is because it is a participation in God's freedom, who needs nothing and desires only good. If baptism calls us to lives of love and self-giving, it is because it brings us into the life of God, who is nothing other than self-giving love, the Father, Son, and Spirit pouring themselves out like libation offerings each one to the others without remain.

With this gift – of incorporation into Christ and participation in the life he shares with the Father and Spirit – comes another: *we* are baptized, and therefore forever belong to one another in Christ, whose Body we are. Christian lives are not meant to be lived individually, but corporately. We need one

JONATHAN JONG

another in the way that a body's organs do, as St Paul recognized (1 Cor. 12.12–27). And we are *baptized*: the verb is
passive; we do not baptize ourselves, but one another. This is
why the idea that we should only be baptized if and when we
fully understand what it is, and choose it for ourselves is just a
misunderstanding of baptism, and indeed, of the Christian life.
Baptism is not something we do, is not our accomplishment.
Furthermore, we never fully understand what baptism is; not
me, not you, not the Pope, not an infant brought before God's
people to be God's people. In this we are on equal footing. And
so we stand – shoulder to shoulder; arms linked; ready to pick
each other up and dust each other off should ever we fall; ever
having each others' backs – we stand and walk together, live
together this impossible life of giving up our lives for the sake
of the world.

This gift of one another is an eminently practical one, then.
It is a gift that acknowledges human frailty and fallibility,
and which also celebrates the mutual interdependence of
human life. It is not just that the *Christian* life is to be lived
corporately, but *human* life, which turns out to amount to the
same thing. Our baptisms bring us closer to God, but we are
baptized into Christ's humanity just as we are into his divinity. The latter does not destroy the former, as if divinity and
humanity are contradictories, but fulfils it: the new creation is
the old creation after all, consummated. This humanity into
which we are baptized – that is, *true* humanity – is far from
the fulfilment of the self-sufficient economically-rational indi-
vidualism that so many of us have imbibed. Rather, it is the
humanity imagined throughout the biblical witness, whenever
it says that it is not good for us to be alone (Gen. 2.18) and
that two are better than one and a threefold cord is not quickly
broken (Eccles. 4.9–12) and that one day we will live peaceably
together, even the wolves and lambs among us, the leopards
and kids, the calves and the bear cubs (Isa. 11.6–9), strange
bedfellows made true by God's transforming power.

It is, in other words and at risk of being trite, humanity
defined not by the markers sought by paleoanthropologists

64

and even many theologians – our allegedly unique abilities to use and innovate tools, our felicity with language, our intellectual and imaginative faculties – but by love, both our need for love and our capacity to love others. Love is, in the end, the nature and function of humanity, made as we are in God's image and baptized as we are into God's name.

Questions for further reflection

• Should all churches practice full immersion baptism?
• Why has the baptism of infants proved controversial in Christian history?
• What is the relationship between baptism and the institutional church?

Further reading

Everett Ferguson, 2013, *Baptism in the Early Church: History, Theology, and Liturgy in the First Five Centuries*, Grand Rapids, MI: William B. Eerdmans.

Herbert McCabe, 2010, *The New Creation*, London: Continuum.

Bryan D. Spinks, 2006, *Early and Medieval Rituals and Theologies of Baptism: From the New Testament to the Council of Trent*, London: Routledge.

World Council of Churches, 1982, *Baptism, Eucharist and Ministry: Faith and Order paper No. 111*, Geneva: World Council of Churches.

6

Love in Thanksgiving:
An Invitation to the Eucharist

PETER GROVES

Presence

The sacrament of the Eucharist takes its name from the Greek verb 'to give thanks'. This thanksgiving, in which Christians share by the offering and receiving of bread and wine, is an action which looks both backwards and forwards. It commemorates the Last Supper, the meal taken on the night before Jesus died, in which he took the bread and the cup and gave them to his disciples with the words 'This is my body' and 'This is my blood'. In this act of memory, Christians are telling the story not just of that meal but of the passion of Christ, indeed of the whole act of divine redemption by which God unites humanity to God's own self in the life, death and resurrection of Jesus. But this act of memory is also an act of presence, a celebration of the essential truth that the activity of God is never enclosed in the past, because the God who meets us in Jesus Christ is present to the world at every moment of its existence. The sacraments represent and celebrate particular forms of that presence, and chief among them is the Eucharist, the sacrament by which God makes truly present the Body and the Blood of Christ.

To be drawn into the presence of Christ is to be called by God, and, as we saw when considering the incarnation as the basis of the sacramental life, God's call is a call to the love and service personified in Jesus. Being nourished by Christ himself, human beings are set apart by God for his purpose, renewed as sacramental beings who take that which God offers and continue that offering in the mission of the Church – bringing Christ to the world in loving action and joyful proclamation.

When Christians talk of the Body of Christ, they are talking of more than one thing. The Church is the called Body of Christ and in that sense means the coming together of the many millions who make up the people of God, in heaven as well as on earth. But the Body of Christ also refers to the coming together of humanity in all its material and physical limitations, with the boundless and inexhaustible love of God. That coming together is what we call the incarnation, and it is celebrated and shown forth every time the holy sacrifice of thanksgiving which we call the Eucharist is offered.

It is vital to recognize that neither of those applications of embodiment, neither meaning of the body of Christ, is something abstract. The body of Christ is far from abstract. It is real, and it is particular. As was insisted when discussing the sacraments, Christianity is not about abstracts, it is about things, and in this case about the particular redeeming presence of God in Jesus Christ, divine and human. It is precisely because of our inability to articulate the meaning of what it is to be divine that God comes among us and transforms our world – and within it, the things that we say – to unite it with the divine. The presence of Christ, which the Eucharist proclaims, is not something static, something limited to an object or a place. It is the presence among us of the eternal offering of the Son to the Father. What is celebrated in the Eucharist is our being drawn up into the worship of heaven, our being enabled to share in the very life of God, a life of perfect self-giving love, the life which we call Father, Son and Holy Spirit.

This is not to say that the Eucharist allows us to get God under control, to reduce the divine presence to something mundane. Proper study of the Christian doctrine of the Eucharist reminds us that the presence of Christ in the sacrament is not a physical, local presence – we are no nearer to Christ at the altar than we are to the north pole, and the body of Christ is not moved as we carry it around. The body of Christ cannot be physically contained, limited or constrained. But although Christ's body has no physical limitation, our bodies do. Our bodies are all we have with which to respond to God's gift and God's mission. It is for this reason that many Christians practise what is called 'eucharistic adoration', forms of worship which draw upon the sacrament of the body and blood of Christ as a focus for prayer which rejoices in the miracle of God's love while also trying to draw closer to that love by offering ourselves to God. But more widely, the Christian response to Christ's eucharistic presence is itself always a bodily response, because it is as ourselves, as particular examples of human bodies, that we are enabled to serve one another, to seek Christ in the needs of his world, and to employ our bodies in his service and the service of those other bodies which we call our human family.

Life

In an important passage of John's Gospel, Jesus speaks of eating his flesh and drinking his blood. Greek teachers enjoy reminding students that the word used here does not mean 'eats' so much as 'munches'. The material reality of the Eucharist, something physical which is something spiritual, could hardly be more clearly stated. But the point of the word is not an emphasis on realism so much as an emphasis on life. The word really belongs in the context of animals feeding, or grazing. For livestock to graze on something is continually to be digesting it, to be sustained by that process of chewing and eating which is the basis of their life. That sixth chapter of John reminds us that the Eucharist is the source of true life. What is present to us in the eucharistic elements is the personal presence of the one who is always and perfectly interceding for all of humanity. In the eucharistic celebration, we present to God our unworthy offering in order that it be taken by Christ and transformed into his perfect offering. Having been transformed, it is given back to the worshipper as the food by which the life of the Church, the Body of Christ, is sustained, the food which is indeed our daily bread.

The miracle of the Eucharist is the miracle of God's creative act, because in order for us to live, to exist at all, we depend entirely on the creative love of God. The story of redemption is the story of that love lived out in a human life, offered once and for all in the whole of the life, death and resurrection of Christ, so that human life can at last fulfil its destiny and enjoy the communion with God for which it was created. That new life is not something future, but something present, and it is given to us day by day and week by week in the miracle of the Eucharist. We depend on the love of God, on the broken body of Christ, for our very lives.

In the midst of life we are in death, as the liturgy tells us. But it is also true that in the midst of death we are in life. And this is so not simply because human beings do show remarkable abilities to love and to help each other, though that is important. Rather, the Christian life is always eternal life, life beyond death, because the ability to love and to serve is the very image of God in humanity – the same outpouring of love which we see incarnated in Jesus Christ and given as the life of the world in the sacrament of the Eucharist.

The intrinsic connection between the celebration of the Eucharist and the wider Christian life can be drawn out in as many different ways as there are instances of Christian service. The history of the Church of England provides a simple and obvious example. From the Reformation onwards it was entirely commonplace for English Christians to receive communion only three or four times a year, but with the more catholic understanding of Anglicanism which the nineteenth century brought, there came a rediscovery of the centrality of the Eucharist to Christian identity. The direct connection between the frequent celebration of the Eucharist and the ministry and mission of God's Church in and for the needs of the world, had been emphasized by many seeking to renew the church, among them the Wesleys in the previous century. Gradually this emphasis took hold and in the 1840s, the first daily celebration of the Eucharist in the Church of England came at the request of a community of religious sisters at Devonport, women ministering in the awful slums of the Plymouth docks during the devastation of the cholera epidemics. God's gift of the Eucharist is to be enjoyed, not protected or held back. As it is sometimes rather flippantly put, Jesus said 'I am the bread of life' he did not say 'I am the jam doughnut of life'. The Eucharist is basic to the Christian life.

When considering what eucharistic life might be, we begin with God's presence among us. That presence is celebrated in the liturgical actions which both frame and constitute the great acts of thanksgiving and communion which are the eucharistic offering. In the twentieth century, a significant revival in scholarly understanding of those acts led to the observation that there are four basic component parts of the eucharistic action, four dramatic signs which play out the presence of the body and blood of Christ. They are found in the Gospel stories of the Last Supper and in the surviving liturgical texts of the earliest Christian communities. When instituting the Eucharist at the Last Supper, Jesus took bread, blessed it, broke it and gave it. This fourfold action – taking, blessing, breaking and giving – is then a model for the Christian life which responds to God's self-gift to us.

Taking

The first of these actions – taking – reminds us that all eucharistic life is God's first, and ours as a result of God's gift. The taking which begins the sacramental action is God's initiative. God 'takes' or 'assumes' humanity in the incarnation, God places humanity in a particular relationship with God's own life, a relationship which allows and enables humanity to be all that humanity was created to be. So when we ask ourselves what it means to 'take' in eucharistic life, we are asking ourselves what God has done already to empower us as Christians.

We 'take' because first of all we acknowledge who God is and how it is that we are in a position to know and to love God: it is because we are first known and loved by God. We are able to understand who we are because we are given to understand who God is in Jesus Christ.

But the eucharistic life God gives is not ours individually. We are taken by God for God's purposes so that we can take the world around us for those same purposes, we can situate ourselves and our lives in the particular needs and actions of the communities of which we are a part. We take ourselves, discerning and rejoicing in the gifts which God has given us, and we take the opportunities which God offers us to make ourselves signs of grace. The Eucharist makes us part of the living Body of Christ, and the Body of Christ, his presence in the world, is always gifted, always dynamic. The eucharistic life, then, must be a life of doing.

And that doing is something material. The 'matter' of the eucharistic celebration – the bread and the wine – are the particular physical objects through which God chooses to work in this individual sacramental action. They are taken, so as to be blessed, broken and given. Likewise, we are the physical stuff taken by God to enact God's love in the world God has created, and that world is itself made up of innumerable particular physical things, each one created by God. There is nothing about the world which is beyond the scope of divine love. When we 'take' that for which we are called to live, we are taking everything that we encounter in the life, loves, fears and struggles of every individual bit of stuff we call creation. The Eucharist is practical thanksgiving – the response of love to the gift of love which works itself out in the real lives of real people.

Blessing

This life, and this action, taken by God to be offered to and taken by us, is a life we are unable to lead if left to ourselves. In telling the story of our salvation, the dramatic action of the

Eucharist blesses those who participate in it, nourishes them with life far beyond that of physical constraint, and sends them out to be a blessing for the world around them. Historians argue as to the precise derivation of the English word 'mass', but the most widely accepted suggestion is that the term comes from the liturgy itself, from the final words of the eucharistic celebration in Latin – *Ite, missa est* (literally, 'Go, it has been sent'), and is closely related to the word 'mission' (from the Latin verb 'to send'). There is a sense in which the eucharistic action is never quite complete, because those who are blessed with the presence of Christ are also sent to bless all else they encounter.

The well-known story of Jesus feeding the five thousand sees a symbol of the eucharistic action in the work of power which transforms five loaves and two fishes into a meal for many thousands of people. Jesus takes the food, blesses, breaks and distributes it to those who are hungry. The act of blessing effects not simply the transformation of the physical food, but the transformation of a basic human action – that of sharing a meal – into something which both symbolizes and contains the grace of God poured out upon those many hundreds who hung on every word of Jesus. Likewise, the Eucharist blesses all our actions by transforming us into the Body of Christ, empowering us to be God's people, God's hands and feet and voice in every place of human need.

If such a claim sounds rather too ambitious for the ordinary Christian lives which each of us struggles to live, we do well to remember that those ordinary lives are only Christian because God has already blessed them, has already made them God's own in the sacrament of baptism. By feeding us with his Body and Blood, Christ blesses all our attempts to be Christ like, those attempts that are successful and the far greater number of attempts which fall flat. To live a eucharistic life is already to have been blessed, and so the tiniest and most simple act of kindness which we manage to achieve is doubly a blessing: a blessing, in that it is a good gift to another, and a blessing because it is a working out of what God has made true of us, and is now making true of the person with whom we interact, with whom we recreate our relationship for God's good purpose. We are giving thanks in what we do for what God has done and we are enabled so to give thanks by that very act of blessing which gives life to our all too feeble attempts to love those we encounter.

Breaking

Christians call the Eucharist a sacrifice and in so doing they are making a rich variety of claims. First of all, they are reminding themselves that the Scriptures know no better way of relating God's decisive redemptive act in Christ than re-imagining the notion of sacrifice inherited in Jewish tradition and locating it within God's outpouring of love for the world. Secondly, they are reclaiming that language of sacrifice for themselves by insisting that what God is doing in the Eucharist is making something holy, which is what our English word sacrifice literally means. God's gift of himself to the world in the incarnation of Christ is the ultimate sacrifice because it is the making holy of everything which is made, the transformation of created stuff into that which is set apart for God.

But the Eucharist is also a sacrifice because it is something which is offered, and it is offered as a retelling and a representation of the offering of himself which Christ makes in his death and resurrection. That offering is not a divine act of fiat, but rather the submission of love to the power of fear and hatred, the embracing of suffering beyond our imagining within God's very life by virtue of the incarnation. To live a eucharistic life of service must be to be broken as well as to be blessed.

So it is that the Christian is not called to separate themselves from the reality of evil and violence in our world: quite the opposite. The Eucharist commemorates an act of violence upon the divine, we are drawn by God into the cosmic drama of the broken body of Christ. That lacerated and bleeding

flesh, pummelled and pierced and hung to its lifeless end, is
the source of the divine life with which we enjoy communion
in the sacrament of the Eucharist. The eucharistic life is never
isolated from the agonies of the world.

But at the same time, the broken body of Christ is transformed into the risen, ascended and glorified body which bears
humanity into the life of God. The death of Christ is not the
end, and the presence of Christ in the Eucharist is not the mag-
ical manifestation of a corpse. Solidarity with those who are
suffering is, for Christians, an extension of the incarnational
solidarity of Christ with all victims of violence and pain. The
breaking which is the vocation of the Christian life is a breaking of ourselves, a willingness to place ourselves in situations
of suffering and need, but also a breaking of the exploitative
greed and power which subjects humans to the evil perpetrated
by other humans. In worshipping God on a cross, Christians
are rejecting a simplistic narrative whereby evil and suffering
have no place: on the contrary, their place is all too real and is
at the heart of Christ's own body. But even as we are called to
solidarity and to endurance, we are also called to hope, in the
knowledge that that which is broken is that which gives life,
and life will ultimately break the power of sin and death.

Giving

The final aspect of our fourfold action returns us to where we
started – to the life of God, which is always to be given to
another in love, and to that life poured out upon the world in
the gift of Jesus Christ. The eucharistic life is a life of giving
because, as with the other actions on which we have reflected,
the act of giving is first of all God's, and secondarily our own.
God gives us the power of gift – gifts to us the true meaning
of giving, in the complete self-giving love which is the life of
the Trinity incarnate in Christ. To celebrate the Eucharist is to
give ourselves to God, but to do so because God has first of all
given God's self to us.

The gift of the Body and Blood of Christ is the gift of life. The biological life we all enjoy is ours because of God's gift, and the divine life which is given to us in baptism is the life which transcends the limitations of here and now and me and mine. The eucharistic action is our joining in with the perpetual pouring out of that life, the inexhaustible flow of God's love and grace which is the perpetual offering of the Son to the Father. By uniting our offering with his own, Christ makes the gift of his life into the day-to-day sustenance of Christian faith and action. To live a eucharistic life is to enact Paul's contention that 'it is no longer I who live, but it is Christ who lives in me' (Gal. 2.20).

Life, by its nature, is productive. The gift of Christ's life in the Eucharist makes our Christian lives real, and our Christian lives are taken, blessed, broken and given by God to the world which we are called to serve. Christian lives are given so as to create new life, to be the vehicles of God's constant recreation of the world. Every act of generosity, every instance of meeting the needs of our neighbour, is something creative, something which brings love into being in a new way. Such acts are eucharistic because they are a response of thanks – conscious or otherwise – to the gift of God's love and life which makes any human interaction possible.

God's gift is never less than abundant. 'I came that they may have life, and have it abundantly', says Jesus (John 10.10). The particularity of the eucharistic offering – the bread and wine which is taken and transformed – becomes, in the life of the church, the food which feeds and sustains an infinite outpouring of love, just as those five loaves and two fishes became the food for many thousands. Again, we return to where we started: God's perfect offering of love in the death and resurrection of Christ is a specific act in a person, a time and a place; and it is also the infinite offering of the divine life which knows nothing of degree or limitation. God's giving knows no bounds, and that boundless abundance manifests itself in the countless acts of love which make up the life of the church.

Communion

The traditional phrase 'Holy Communion' sums up beautifully the eucharistic action and its consequences. This is a communion, a sharing, with the divine life. In the incarnation of the Word humanity is taken by God, blessed and made holy by God's presence, broken in the self-offering of God's love and given in and for the new life of Easter which is the fulfilment of creation. The communion which is God's gift in the sacrament of the Eucharist is a sharing in that incarnational offering. Communion with the divine life means being given in love and therefore those who are nourished by the Eucharist are transformed by the presence of Christ into sacraments of his love, ministers who themselves take, bless, break and give their lives in the service of God and of others. To be a Christian is to live the Eucharist.

Questions for further reflection

- How do the various meanings of 'the body of Christ' relate to one another?
- What is the significance of God's coming among us in the context of food?
- Why has the issue of Christ's 'presence' been so very controversial in Christian history?

Further reading

Thomas O'Loughlin, 2015, *The Eucharist: Origins and Contemporary Understandings*, London: Bloomsbury.
Alexander Schmemann, 1997, *The Eucharist: Sacrament of the Kingdom*, Yonkers, NY: St Vladimir's Seminary Press.
John Macquarrie, 1997, *A Guide to the Sacraments*, London: SCM Press.

7

Love in Proclamation:
An Invitation to Evangelism
and Mission

MELANIE MARSHALL

When I first realized that I needed to take Christianity seriously, my parish priest did not quiz me on what I believed.
Instead he gave me two pieces of advice. First, he said, take
a prayer book from the back of church and say the psalms
appointed for morning and evening. And then he told me that
the soup kitchen needed volunteers.

Christianity is first and foremost a distinctive way of life.
The Church's mission (from Latin *mitto*, 'I send') is simply to
live that life with as much integrity as we can muster. When
we do this, we continue Christ's work of making God visible
in the world. God provides the initiative and model for this
when God enters God's own creation as a human being, Jesus
of Nazareth – or as many New Testament authors put it: the
Father 'sends' the Son. The Father sends the Son for a specific
purpose as Jesus points out: 'For this I was born, and for this I
came into the world, to testify to the truth' (John 18.37), and
Jesus fulfils God's mission perfectly. Because he is God as well
as a human being, his whole life, death and resurrection – what
we sometimes call 'the Christ event' – reflect the truth of who
God is. The truth Jesus reveals is a God who exists eternally to
give, heal, restore, attend and do no violence.

Jesus chose followers to continue his work of revealing the
God of peace: 'As the Father has sent me, so I send you' (John

20.21). This is a big risk. The apostles (from Greek *apostello*, 'I send out') are only human. The seventy or so men whom Jesus sent out to the towns and villages of Galilee have not even had the benefit of witnessing the resurrection but Jesus trusts them with this extraordinary mission all the same. After the resurrection the disciples come to realize that their friend and master Jesus is really God. The risen Jesus leads the twelve up the mountain where they worshipped him. But they also had doubts (Matt. 28.17). They felt confident of Jesus's divinity. What they felt far from confident about was their own capacity for making God known.

The apostles' misgivings may seem odd and even discouraging. Why send people on a mission if they are not completely sure of themselves? Surely we want the most capable and persuasive advocates for the gospel. On the contrary. Our mission is to have full confidence in God and put no trust in ourselves. Christians are just like everyone else. We have the same shabby motivations and the same lazy preference for our own comfort. We are as complicit as anyone in the world's cruelty and indifference to suffering. If we happen to be articulate or hardworking or clever we are in danger of using these gifts not to make God known but to promote ourselves and win approval from other people, whether their approval is really worth having or not. Jesus did not choose as his apostles the smart or elegant, the wealthy or perfectly pious. He chose and goes on choosing people who have the same shortcomings and weaknesses as everyone else. The difference is only that we know it. Knowing Jesus shows us how far we are from being perfect. It also shows us that human life can be lived not according to our usual priorities but in imitation of God's love, and that when we do that all kinds of unforeseen flourishing begins. In this chapter we'll see how the Church's mission is characterized by the habits of repentance, listening and service. We live like this not mainly to convert people but because Christ shows us that's what a truly human life should be. If others see it and decide they too want to live in this more excellent way, God and Christ's Church welcome them with open arms.

What if I'm wrong?

A friend of mine, a very capable senior administrator, has a sign above her desk. It reads simply "What if I'm wrong?" In his earthly ministry, Jesus encountered a lot of people who were convinced that they were right and who acted energetically out of that conviction. From the Pharisees stoning the woman taken in adultery to the future St Paul breathing threats and violence against the church, none of these zealots emerges in a good light. Each story tells the same tale. As long as they are sure they are right, their minds are closed. They are not open to relationship with Jesus nor with the God who made and loves them, let alone with other people around them. Happily, most of the stories show these characters repenting. They turn around, change their minds, take a new direction. The first thing Jesus says in his earthly ministry is not (as is often claimed) 'repent'. It is 'get repenting'. Not 'change your mind once and for all, and then you really will be in the right at last'. But rather 'begin the process of changing your mind, of acknowledging how little you know and how often you'll have to admit you're wrong. Get into the habit of it.' And yes, the Greek language can encapsulate that difference in a single word!

Repentance is a constant and necessary part of the Christian way of life. It begins in baptism, when we turn away from evil and towards Christ, and continues at every celebration of the eucharist. The Church's thanksgiving cannot begin until we have first collectively confessed our sins and received God's forgiveness. In the sacrament of reconciliation the priest offers personal counsel and the assurance of God's mercy after listening in detail to a penitent's sins. The wise Christian will make confession regularly, but even those who don't will say the Lord's prayer at least once a day. The words 'Forgive us our sins as we forgive those who sin against us' are never far from a Christian's lips. Repentance offers freedom and new life. There are two distinct groups of people who can benefit from this: those who know they are wrong, and those who know they are right.

Let's begin with those who know they are wrong. The first decades of the twenty-first century have been characterized by many public demands for repentance, apology and reparation. The catalogue of past and present outrages is almost inexhaustible and has spawned a depth of grievance which it sometimes feels can never be assuaged. As well as the horrors of slavery and child molestation, the Church's missionary history has come under particular scrutiny. European missions of the colonial era did not invariably display contempt or indifference towards the host culture but they often did. Economic and political motives may not always have been overt or conscious but they were rarely absent. Missionaries condemned violence and they perpetuated it too. More than one sentence is owed to the bravery, wisdom and generosity of many foreign missionaries, without whom countless languages would not have been recorded and countless schools and hospitals never built. Nonetheless, it was as apparent in the nineteenth and twentieth centuries as it is to us now that predatory colonialism and missionary endeavour far too often moved in step.

Of the many agencies involved in these kinds of malfeasance, the Church should be the very first to repent. In baptism we die with Christ and rise with him and so have already lost everything – face, status, authority, life. We have received an identity that is not dependent on anything in this world and certainly not on being right. We can turn away from evil and do good in the knowledge that we have nothing to lose and our souls to gain by doing so. More than this, we have a ministry to others who are wrong. Anyone will hold up their hands to complicity in our colonial past. Other kinds of transgression present a greater temptation to evade any real admission of wrongdoing. In our media age, public figures and organizations of all kinds are up to the neck in elaborate and dishonest forms of face-saving. Most alarming of all is when the Church seems to be going the same way, with even bishops unable to utter a simple 'I was wrong and I'm sorry'. Yet such candour is a crucial part of the Church's mission. We want to return to the Lord who will have mercy. We have also been sent to model

God's loving welcome for others who know they have messed up. What hope is there for former prisoners, and for the many people oppressed by their own failings and the harm they have caused, if there is no one in the world to show that being wrong is not the end of everything? The Church's mission is to offer the hope that only comes from receiving forgiveness.

As for those who know they are right, they probably need repentance even more. There is a moral danger in denouncing people, which can easily trap us in self-righteousness and lead us into dehumanizing outrage and polarized views of others. In our current debates we often find ourselves too wary to point this out but a Desert Father of the early Church put it bluntly: 'We have put aside the easy burden which is self-accusation and weighed ourselves down with the heavy burden which is self-justification' (John the Dwarf in Ward, p. 42). No one is right all the time and we often try to disguise this from ourselves by pointing the finger at others' shortcomings or occupying the moral high ground of victimhood. Christ's way is different. He was content to fail and die rather than join in these frightened power-games. Christians too are called to be a people who can never know that we are absolutely right – let alone 'in the right', that most malignant of standpoints. Our righteousness comes from outside us. It is not something we own but something we are always in the process of receiving. A nun writing to a newspaper to take issue with an article ended her letter 'but perhaps I have misunderstood or the error is my own'. In a culture of toxic certainty, our mission is to hold open a space for the unknown, for another reality. Jesus said, 'No one is good but God alone' (Luke 18.19). If we're human we could always be wrong. And yet we are held in God's love all the same. This life-saving freedom is for everyone, and we are sent to model it.

Listening to God, listening to others

If the Church is going to show people God, it must first get to know God and get to know God's people. If we understood our mission to be only this – listening to God and listening to others – we would already be making a radical and visible counter-cultural statement. Next to no one listens to God and the typical discourse of the twenty-first century is almost defined by a failure to listen to others. Social media in particular encourage us to relate to one another as a set of disembodied opinions encapsulated in 140 characters or fewer. It is increasingly normal to think that there is only one valid perspective and that those who disagree or raise concerns must be humiliated and annihilated as enemies of truth. By contrast, the Gospels show Jesus listening all the time both to God and to other people. We can't expect to be perfect in our listening as Jesus is. But we undertake to embrace silence and the humble obedience to our Maker that emerges from making room in our lives for God's transcendent perspective.

Prayer is radical in two ways. First, it is the practice of simply existing. The creature undertakes to set aside time to just be and nothing else in the presence of the Creator. The Creator simply exists in the creature's presence in turn. Prayer is a riotous and time-wasting celebration of the absolutely priority of Being, both human and divine. The praying Christian is a sign to the world that our true self is given, not bought or made or earned. By contrast, if there is one thing that characterizes the false self constructed by materialism, it is doing. Working, getting, spending, consuming, discarding, improving, upgrading, replacing, performing are all ways of trying to establish that we have value. This is a mistake. We have infinite value just by being children of a loving Father. Prayer turns its back on a culture of anxious acquisition and display, revelling instead in simple being – something dangerously free in both senses of the word. Second, prayer reminds us that we are not God. It exposes us to and aligns us with a narrative that is not of our choice or making. In the conscious presence of God we can't avoid the reality that God is the maker of heaven and earth and everything in them. God's very existence is a refusal of party or privilege. God sends the sun on the righteous and the unrighteous alike. Christians – if we are to be worthy of the name – cannot claim a resting place of settled moral security. Indeed, we are the very last people who can do that. We have relinquished any moral law besides love. We have no rule-book to assure us we are on the right side of God or neighbour. We undertake to live in Christ's Spirit, a spirit of encounter, connection and anarchic love.

This means that mission and evangelism can't be undertaken with a fixed outcome in mind. We are sent to do the exact opposite of what 'a man with a mission' and 'evangelical' mean colloquially. Guiding people deeper into the embrace of their loving Maker can never be a goal, a statistic, a box to tick. And yet our egos rebel against anything as open-ended as the Spirit at work. Thomas the apostle is famous for complaining that he can't be expected to know the way without first knowing the destination (John 14.5). Jesus corrects him. If we are faithful to the way – that is, to Jesus himself – the destination will take care of itself. This is a hard saying. We prefer to fixate on the destination, whether it's numbers of candidates for confirmation or numbers in the pews, converting one tricky person or stirring up a stadium to hysteria. Outcomes reassure us we're succeeding, in the world's terms at least, and soon any method will do to achieve them. Persuade, flirt, cajole, browbeat, harangue. Stand on a street corner denouncing sin and calling down hellfire. Subtly humiliate those with questions. Convince people that there is only one way of thinking: ours. When others choose it, it vindicates our scary choices. When other people are (or seem) convinced, our own doubts and misgivings are assuaged – at least for a time.

As Jesus says: 'It will not be so among you' (Matt. 20.26). When his disciples wanted to be top dog, they misunderstood the God they were sent to make visible. Violence can be overt or subtle, and may be physical, verbal, emotional or mental, but as soon as it enters the scene, God has fled. Our insistence or manipulation have hidden the One who only ever offers and welcomes. Our attempts to put others down have fatally distorted the image of the One who only ever builds up. The great twentieth-century philosopher Simone Weil said that if we are faced with a choice between betraying Christ and betraying the truth, we should always betray Christ. She meant that God is the truth. God does not need us anxiously defending our distorted version of him and we only make ourselves look foolish when we try. By contrast, if you have ever seen the former Archbishop Rowan Williams in debate, you will know that he always wins. He does this not by trouncing the arguments of his opponents, but by honouring them. By his graciousness and by the seriousness and respect he shows his interlocutors, he makes visible Christ's attentive love and the gentleness that is the fruit of Christ's Spirit. That Spirit conquered even death and hell. The violence of Christ's killers achieved nothing.

No surprise, then, that the Lord's whole earthly ministry was a ministry of listening. Jesus was often found in debate and he always dealt deftly, wittily and gently with his interlocutors however far from the truth they may have seemed. Likewise when he heals or feeds or reunites outcasts with their community or brings people back from the dead, it always begins with listening. He never forces anyone. Remember that the rich young man walked sadly away – and Jesus didn't stop him (Matt. 19.16–22). But if someone is asking for new life he hears them and gives it in exactly the form they need. We are sent to be as Christ in the world. Imagine if our interactions with others, whatever the subject, took the form 'I'd like to understand exactly how you feel and why. Please take as long as you need. If I can help, I will. I am listening.' What then?

Well, we may lose the chance to get across that compelling version of the gospel we're so proud of having crafted. What a relief! Philosophical arguments for the existence of God only convince people who already believe in God. Over-simplified versions of Christian doctrine do violence to the richness of Christ's self-offering and insult the intelligence of the hearer.

Sometimes we do need words, of course. There are universal human questions about origins and destinies and purposes and the gospel's answers need to be voiced. Jesus promises that the Holy Spirit will be the one to give us those words and that he will give them only in the moment – that is, in response to particular human need. Many of these words have come down to us and the Spirit has bestowed on the church quite a bank of scriptural and other prayerful wisdom to call on. But they are only part of our mission when they are used to answer another's need, not to satisfy our own. In the person of Jesus, God speaks exactly the saving Word his children need to hear. Our Lord does not waste words. Nor should we.

Service

Our Lord got to his knees and washed the feet of his disciples, a job for the lowest of the low among the household slaves. This is a far cry from the Church's patchy history, which has at times included complicity in accruing vast wealth by dubious means and political power-games at the highest level. But in Western Europe at least the position of Christians is no longer straightforwardly hegemonic. Our ideology is unpopular. The Church's ties to power and even influence are loosening. If anything, the authentically Christian life today is marked by visible resistance to the privileges that come from economic and political advantage.

Nonetheless, many of us continue to benefit from the exploitation that is the basis of much of the world's wealth. It is not through our chosen identity as Christians but through our default identity as consumers that we continue the work of degrading our brothers and sisters. We are not separate from the polity we live in, not unless we really are Shakers. Our taxes pay for the arms trade just like everyone else. But we can make choices in how we vote, what we eat and wear, the way we talk to and about other people, and how we save and spend our money. Sacrificing time and energy and our shallow preferences and conveniences and choosing instead to give attention to the real conditions under which things are made or sold or financed – that is a mark of Christian life. We will certainly fail. This is both because our markets often do not offer us any truly ethical options, and because there are human limits to our vigilance and effort. We are works in progress, constantly being remade in God's image. The process is slow and halting by which our lives and bodies becomes witnesses to the beauty and durability of what God offers: solidarity and compassion and new life, things realer than fleeting material comfort for a lucky few.

We should not be discouraged by slow progress. We are sent not to build a whole new world, but to point to a parallel universe, a kingdom of justice which already exists and is very near us. As such, it is what we do day by day that constitutes the greatest part of the Church's lived mission. Some Christians are called to be campaigners against the death penalty or medics in war zones, to offer a home to a child with complex needs or live as a silent hermit. But this kind of service – the kind that attracts television documentaries – is relatively unusual. Most of us are called to quite ordinary lives. The Church's mission is mainly seen in delivering food parcels and visiting lonely people, in projects as dull as installing toilets and central heating in church buildings. A former bishop of Oxford was lambasted for suggesting that the point of Church of England schools was not to primarily evangelize the nation's children, but to serve them and their families by offering quality education for free. He was absolutely right. Service is not glamorous. Neither is it part of a heroic narrative of victory for our party. Service is showing ordinary human care in sex offender wings, and to people living with hopeless debt or devastating disability or terrible addiction. God's non-judgemental love is a scandal. God sends us to scandalize the world.

What then will we have?

As it dawned on the first disciples what was being asked of them, they started to quaver. Who wouldn't? In Christ God called them to lose everything – their superiority and sense of being right, their confidence in their own opinions and understanding, their safety and security and material wealth, even their lives. Christians are called to be the world's losers. For the most part living as Christians will make us negligible, people to whom the world pays no attention. If it does happen that our distinctiveness attracts notice, we have no way of predicting how it will be received. An atheist secular society with an acquisitive mindset is a hard place to live Christ's way. To a few people perhaps his way will be beautiful, enticing, intriguing. It is more likely to be considered baffling or enraging, ridiculous or pathetic.

It doesn't matter. Our home is not here. This is just where we are posted, a crack squad of carers and listeners and forgivers and peacemakers, sent to infiltrate a fallen world with the powerful reality of subversive love. That is our mission should we choose to accept it. The bad news is that it will kill us, but the good news is that we can't ever be separated from the source of that love, the gift that keeps on giving to the end of the age and beyond. Our spell on earth is just one tiny moment in God's universal masterplan to win the world over to love. If our little mission is aborted rather sooner than we'd hoped, that puts us in good company. Jesus only had 33 years on the planet and only three of active ministry. The playwright Samuel Beckett was once asked when he would write his next full-length play. 'All my plays are full-length', he said. Whether our lives in Christ are long or short, we are called to be filled with all the fullness of God, showing the world the breadth and length and height and depth of Christ's love. That love can accomplish in us abundantly far more than all we can ask or imagine. There is not a single minute to lose.

Questions for further reflection

- What does it mean to live in a way that makes others ask about the source of your hope and motivation?
- What would it look like for repentance to be a constant and necessary part of your life? What about listening as a constant and necessary part of your life? Or prayer? Or service?
- How do you hold space open in your life for God?
- What does it mean for you that 'Christians are called to be the world's losers'?

Bibliography

Benedicta Ward (trans.), 1984, *The Sayings of the Desert Fathers: The Alphabetical Collection*, revised ed., Kalamazoo, MI: Cistercian Publications.

Further reading

Al Barrett and Ruth Harley, 2020, *Being Interrupted: Reimagining the Church's Mission from the Outside, In*, London: SCM Press.

Simon Cuff, 2020, *Only God Will Save Us: The Nature of God and the Christian Life*, London: SCM Press.

A. D. A. France-Williams, 2020, *Ghost Ship: Institutional Racism and the Church of England*, London: SCM Press.

Rowan Williams, 2004, *Silence and Honey Cakes: The Wisdom of the Desert*, Oxford: Lion.

8

Love in Self-Gift:
An Invitation to Justice and
Reconciliation

JONATHAN JONG

Christianity is often recognized by scholars of religion as a
'religion of salvation', which is one that diagnoses a fundamental
problem in creation and offers a solution. For example, the
major Indian religions – Buddhism, Hinduism, Sikhism and
Jainism – are concerned with freedom from *saṃsāra*, the endless cycle of life, death and rebirth that is, by its nature, laden
with suffering. This freedom, most commonly called *moksha*
and *nirvāṇa*, is described in various ways, including the extinc-
tion of the self, the elimination of desire and oneness with all
existence.

Christians believe that people need to be saved from sin and
death, and that Jesus Christ has accomplished the saving deed.
As in the case of Indian religions, though, we also talk about
salvation in a variety of ways. Sometimes, a legal metaphor is
used: sin is a crime that carries a penalty, which Christ suffers
on our behalf. Sometimes, an economic metaphor is used: sin is
a debt we owe, which Christ pays for us. Sometimes, a medical
metaphor is used: sin is a disease, from which Christ heals us.
In the Bible as well as in subsequent Christian writings, these
and still other ways of thinking about salvation have been
developed into what theologians call 'theories of atonement',
all of which have their virtues but also their limitations.

Atonement is a word whose etymology is hidden in plain sight, being a compound of at-one-ment, referring to a state of persons being in agreement, accord or unity. History buffs might appreciate the irony that Thomas More and William Tyndale – certainly not at one with each other in life – are both credited for coining the word, though its theological usage is certainly due more to the latter, who introduced it to English translations of the Bible.

The fact that we use this word when talking about salvation is significant, as it implies something about what we think lies behind our metaphors and theories. For Christians, to be saved is to be at one with God or, more specifically, to be reconciled with God. Indeed, if asked to pick a single verse from the Bible that summarizes the Christian faith, we could do much worse than to choose 2 Corinthians 5.19: 'in Christ God was reconciling the world to himself'.

The reconciliation parables

It is sometimes said that Christianity is not a religion, but a relationship. While the implied opposition is facile, it is certainly true that Christianity must be understood in relational terms, and especially in familial terms. When teaching us to pray, Jesus tells us to call God our Father (Matt. 6.9–13; Luke 11.2–4) and this sense that through Christ we have become God's children is echoed throughout the New Testament (e.g., John 1.12; Rom. 8.14–16; Gal. 3.26; 1 John 3.1). It is also no accident that the parable of the prodigal son (Luke 15.11–32) occupies such a prominent place in the Christian imagination.

The parable of the prodigal son is a story about reconciliation, of course, and is commonly read as the gospel in dramatic miniature. It tells of a son's rebellion against his father, which ends with the father receiving him home with open arms. There are obvious parallels here with perhaps the most influential way of narrating the Christian story of salvation, which involves a primordial fall from grace as well as a gracious invitation to return to the Father's embrace. Crucially, in both cases, reconciliation is a gift, and wholly undeserved. In the parable, the prodigal son does offer to return as a labourer rather than as an heir, as if in recompense, but this offer is refused by the father who instead lavishes upon him finery and feasting. And so it is that Christians have always maintained that it is God alone who accomplishes our reconciliation.

As compelling as it is and as popular as it has been, the parable is – like all parables – imperfect, which Luke's Gospel acknowledges in its inclusion of other parables. It is imperfect in at least two related ways. First, it fails – unlike the parables of the lost sheep and lost coin that precede it in Luke's Gospel – to say anything about what the father did, if anything, to find his estranged son. As far as we can tell, he does nothing but stare out the window waiting, only running out when his son is in sight. In stark contrast, we are told that the woman who has lost her coin lights a lamp and sweeps the house and the man who has lost a sheep heads out into the wilderness and carries it home. These two stories provide a better sense of God's initiative in our salvation, who after all bridged the impossible distance between heaven and earth to meet us here.

None of these parables really adequately conveys the cost of reconciliation, though the detail about the shepherd risking the safety of ninety-nine sheep for the sake of one gestures in this direction. For Christians, reconciliation is not just a gift, but a gift of God's own self. This point is crucial, not just as a demonstration of divine largesse towards us, but as an expression of what Christians believe about God: that God is nothing other than the Father, Son and Holy Spirit giving themselves wholly to one another. The self-gift of God to us is therefore an invitation to participate in this divine life, and not only an invitation but the means through which we are brought into this life of self-giving.

Reconciliation in Christ

We usually focus on the crucifixion and death of Jesus when we think about God's self-gift: the Cross is our icon of self-sacrificial love, in which the Son offers himself up to the Father for the sake of the world. But the events of Good Friday are the culmination of a life that is entirely a sacrifice, which the hymn in Philippians 2.6–11 describes as self-emptying. Indeed, the change from life to death, even death on the cross, is infinitesimal compared to that between divinity and humanity, which is simply inconceivable. It is this ultimate sacrifice of God that unites creation to its creator, bridging what seems an infinite divide. God becomes one of us, that we might become one with God.

Christians take this idea of unity with God very far indeed. Reconciliation with God is not to be likened with estrangement resolved between father and son or enmity ended between foes: these are insufficiently intimate as metaphors. Over and over and over again, the New Testament describes Christians as being 'in Christ'. Indeed, for Christians, to be saved is to be incorporated into the body of the one who was raised. Perhaps we have grown familiar with the oft-repeated idea that we are the body of Christ, but we should never lose the sense of closeness that this conveys.

Nor should we lose sight of the implications of being Christ's body – his eyes and ears, his hands and feet (1 Cor. 12.12–27). Christians have always maintained that salvation is a gift from God and not something to be achieved by us through our good behaviour, but it would be wrong to assume that we detach salvation from moral obligation altogether. If to be saved is to participate in the divine life of self-giving through unity with Christ as his body, then it is also to act in accordance with Christ's will, who is our head.

This perspective on what it is to be saved reveals a limitation to theories of atonement that emphasize certain understandings of *substitution* and *satisfaction*, in which Christ has to die in our place to satisfy the requirements of divine justice or even anger. Rather, Christ's offering of himself to God the Father is continuous with the eternal and mutual self-offering that is the life of the Trinity: the difference is that creation – and humanity in particular – is now included in this offering. Far from exempting us from death, Christ's dying on the cross invites and frees us to die with him, not as the wages of our own sin but as self-sacrificial love for others. After all, as we have seen in Chapter 5, we are baptized into the death of Christ as well as his resurrection. Our self-offering is, on this view, therefore not just a reaction to the gift of salvation that is strictly distinct from it, but inherent to what it is to be saved.

Reconciliation as truth-telling

Just as salvation can be described in many ways, so can the working out of our salvation. In the same breath, St Paul describes salvation as reconciliation to God and us as ministers and ambassadors of reconciliation, which has captured the Christian moral imagination ever since (2 Cor. 5.18–20). This notion of Christians as ambassadors of reconciliation has been most salient in two related contexts. The first is in the sacrament of reconciliation, commonly called 'confession'. The second is in the work of restorative justice, such as powerfully developed in truth and reconciliation commissions (TRCs) in South Africa after apartheid and in more than 40 countries since with varying success. Such commissions are not unique to Christian contexts, but it is no coincidence that its architects included two clergymen, Alex Boraine, who was President of the Methodist Church of Southern Africa, and Desmond Tutu, Anglican Archbishop of Cape Town.

At first glance, there might seem to be a chasm between these two cases, which is the difference between the private and the public, the personal and the political. The confessional with its seal is the paragon of privacy, after all, and I do not think it violates any expectations of confidentiality to observe that the sins confessed therein tend to be personal in nature. In contrast, the TRC held public hearings to ensure that South Africans – and indeed, people around the world – were aware of the atrocities of apartheid. These atrocities were committed by individuals, but were also part of a larger policy and programme, enshrined in law. But it is always a mistake to draw too sharp a line between the personal and political, as indeed the South African case demonstrates: policies are carried out by people. And many of our actions as individuals participate in larger systems and structures about which there might be moral truths to be discerned.

Indeed, perhaps the most obvious thing that the sacrament of reconciliation and TRCs share is a concern for truth-telling. In the sacrament, the penitent is required to confess his sins, which is to say that he is to utter truths about himself and what he has done, not least to himself. The work of the priest is also to respond truthfully. It is a dereliction of duty to thoughtlessly prescribe some number of Hail Marys or Our Fathers to every penitent: sometimes – perhaps even often – the act of penitence should involve some work, not least the work of apology, reparation and reconciliation. But even before this work is done, the priest proclaims another truth, which is the truth of God's love and forgiveness. Similarly, the work of restorative justice also involves the laying bare of facts as a prelude to reconciliation. Perpetrators are invited to provide full and truthful accounts of their crimes, and victims are also given the chance to tell their stories of how these crimes have damaged their lives. What happens next differs from context to context, but amnesty might be offered and calls for reparative actions made.

The concern for truth-telling in these situations is a part of a larger pattern, visible throughout the New Testament. We are told that the truth will make us free and that we are to worship the Father in spirit and in truth (John 8.32; John 4.24). We are told that the Church is the pillar and bulwark of the truth, and that Christians are to put away falsehood and speak truth (1 Tim. 3.15; Eph. 4.25). We are told to speak truth in love and to love in truth and action (Eph. 4.15; 1 John 3.18). To be sure, this truth that we are called to proclaim is the truth of the gospel, which is in the first place the truth about the God who loves us and saves us: but it is also the truth about us, and the conditions in which we find ourselves in need of salvation.

In other words, Christians are called to prophetic work, which in our biblical tradition is the work of identifying injustice and idolatry. The caricature of the prophet, whether Jeremiah or John the Baptizer, is not as silly as we might like it to be. We might not be called to fashion a yoke for ourselves as Jeremiah did or to eat locusts as John did, but we are certainly called to confront the world with the truth about itself, even if it costs us our dignity, our safety and our lives. It is odd, perhaps, to remind the Christians to exercise our moral voice in public: after all, many Christians already do this and sometimes we might wish they wouldn't. Make no mistake: our moral judgements are fallible and will sometimes turn out to be false. But this risk is one that we must take because the alternative is silent complicity.

Our moral fallibility is precisely why we need to take the task of moral discernment seriously as part of our religious duty. To be sure, this will involve biblical exegesis and the application of systems of moral theology, but also among our resources is the rich and ambivalent history of Christian moral proclamation, action and inaction. The Church has, even in recent history, campaigned for social welfare reform, international aid and the protection of refugees, and against apartheid, segregation, slavery and war and has also impeded such reforms and abetted, even encouraged, such injustices. It is imperative that we are ourselves confronted with the truth of this history – the exemplary and shameful elements both – and learn from it.

Reconciliation with God and among people

Another apparent gap between the work of restorative justice on one hand and the sacrament of reconciliation on the other is that one seems to be concerned with reconciliation between

people whereas the other seems to be concerned with reconciliation with God. This latter assumption is mistaken; or rather,
the idea that reconciliation with God can be neatly separated
from reconciliation among people is mistaken. For starters –
and again, it breaks no confidences for me to say – most sins
committed, whether confessed or not, are sins that involve
other people. Furthermore, the sins of any one member of
Christ's body harm the whole, no less than a wound on any
part of our bodies affects us more broadly. We have grown
accustomed to think of our faith, including where it interacts
with morality, as a private affair, between ourselves and God
alone: but this view of faith is quite foreign to Christianity,
especially given our view of salvation described above.

Even the parable of the prodigal son contains something of
this idea that reconciliation with God involves reconciliation
with others. Indeed, about a third of the story is about the
elder son's dissatisfaction with the father's reception of his
errant brother, or as he puts it to his father 'this son of yours'
(Luke 15.30). Undeterred, the father reminds him of his own
relationship with the prodigal: 'this brother of yours was dead
and has come to life; he was lost and has been found' (Luke
15.32). The banquet thrown is therefore not only a celebration
but also an occasion for reconciliation: the prodigal is a son
once more and can also be a brother once more. Rather than
telling us that the brothers are finally reunited in love, the story
leaves us to imagine possible endings, which is to say that
it invites us to participate in the ending of enmities and the
building of bonds of love.

The business of ending enmities and healing building bonds
is Christian business, flowing as it does from what our salvation
means. We have already seen this in action in the sacrament of
reconciliation and in TRCs, but there is a lot of space in between
them, which is where most of us live most of the time. There is
a lot of work to be done that gets called by various names like
'mediation' and 'conflict resolution' and 'peace-building' that is
the work of bringing reconciliation to others, and which is the
work to which Christians are called. This work is to be found

in diverse contexts from the geopolitical to the professional to the domestic. Few of us will be invited to chair TRCs, but all of us will encounter troubled relationships of many kinds, and when we are, we should remember that God 'has given us the ministry of reconciliation' (2 Cor. 5.18).

It is, by now, a cliché to observe that we live in fractious times and much attention is paid to the things that divide us. We seem not only to espouse different values, but even cling to different facts, distrusting one another's sources of facts. In such a world, the work of reconciliation is certainly daunting. Our commitment to discerning and speaking the truth matters here, but even that will not suffice to bridge the many gaps that exist in modern societies. The work of listening is crucial too, and necessary for discerning truths about the causes of our divisions and disagreements. Reflecting the wider society in which we exist, the Church – in our various denominational manifestations – is also currently struggling to listen to one another across our theological, moral and political divides. There has been much talk in the Church of England, for example, about 'mutual flourishing' and 'disagreeing well', and while we should not be surprised that progress on this front is slow, nor should we despair, because these are struggles towards reconciliation.

It may not be obvious to anyone, least of all ourselves, that Christians are especially qualified for this work: not only is our history is marked by conflict and schism and war, but our present moment is also rife with internecine battles, especially over matters of gender and sexuality. But our failures do not diminish our obligations one jot. The vocation of the Church to be an embassy of reconciliation is not predicated on its own successes any more than her salvation is. Indeed, as we have already seen, both come from the same place, which is the indefatigable and irresistible love of God who reconciles through self-gift. Nor is our ability to heal wounded relationships contingent upon our ability to heal ourselves. However, if we are indeed now unqualified for this work to which we are called, then our duty is to learn. Whatever the case, the pitfalls to avoid are hubris and hypocrisy on one hand and the dereliction of duty on the other.

No justice, no peace

The slogan 'No justice, no peace' often heard at demonstrations and protests against racism can and has been interpreted in myriad ways. It has been received as a threat, often by those opposing such protests. It has been understood as a lament, about how there can be no peace in hearts broken by violence and injustice. It has been read asymmetrically, but also as expressing the interdependence of justice and peace. Certainly, this was the sense of Martin Luther King Jr's longer version, preached to protestors against the Vietnam War gathered outside Santa Rita prison in California in 1968: 'There can be no justice without peace and there can be no peace without justice'.

Restorative justice does not demand retribution, but it does have justice as its end, including the redistribution of power and wealth. Similarly, the sacrament of reconciliation does not require restitution prior to absolution, but it does demand repentance, which is poorly understood as a synonym for feeling guilty. The call to repentance is, in the New Testament, a call to action and to a different way of life. This is why the rite for the sacrament of reconciliation involves acts of penance (though these are too often reduced to mindless rituals). Again, both cases reflect the logic of salvation, which while not earned by us does make demands of us, inherent to what it means to be reconciled with God.

All of which is to say that the work of reconciliation will in certain times and places require us to work towards justice, which is at least in part work to redress injustice. It is a mistake commonly made to draw too strong a distinction between historic injustices and present inequalities: the latter are very often the offspring of the former. For this reason, the putting right of things as they are now – as well as the mitigation of future injustices – will very often require reparation for past injustices. The Church has recently, and all too gradually, awoken to this reality. As I am writing, the Jesuit Conference of Canada and the United States has just announced a pledge to raise US$100 million in reparative payments to descendants of people the order had enslaved and sold. Similar, albeit smaller, efforts have emerged across the United States. The Church of England has been much slower to move in this direction, despite its complicity in the slave trade and the shameful fact that slave-owners – including clergymen – but not slaves were compensated when slavery was abolished.

There are other historic injustices still – against other ethnic groups and indigenous peoples, against women, against sexual minorities, against the aged, against the indigent – all of which continue to this day, in all of which the Church has been and continues to be complicit. The shape of our repentance is clear, and we should not pretend otherwise: the Church must do penance towards reconciliation, and it will not do simply to recite prayers learnt by rote. It is a costly thing to receive the free gift of God's reconciling work in Christ, being a participant in Christ's own sacrifice. The body of which we have been made members is one forever broken to heal the world, including parts of it which we ourselves have wounded.

There is something fitting in the inextricability of the Church's part in these injustices and everyone else's: the planks in our eyes turn out to be attached to the splinters in those of governments and businesses and other organizations and individuals, and so the work of extracting them is also linked. The work of justice within the Church comes neither before nor after the work of justice in the world, but always together. The indignity of an imperfect Church calling the world to perfection is one to be suffered in humility, a part of our penitential act.

It can be difficult to imagine what individual Christians are supposed to do about all these injustices in the world or even within the Church. We seem powerless. But we are not. So many more of our everyday decisions than we suppose – to speak or not to speak, to act or not to act, to vote or not to vote, to buy or to buy – are decisions for which considerations of justice are relevant. This is perhaps especially true in the democracies and market economies in which so many of us – certainly most readers of this book – live. Just as it is a mistake to confine religion to the thing that one does on Sundays at church, it is a mistake to confine the work of justice to the signing of petitions or financial contributions to organizations that fight for justice. In both cases, the gospel pervades our entire lives. In this way, our repentance and reconciliation are not, as St John Paul II put it, 'lofty abstractions' but 'concrete Christian values to be achieved in our daily lives', by the grace of almighty God.

Questions for further reflection

- Reconciliation with God and reconciliation with other people are inseparable. What does it mean that God has given us the 'ministry of reconciliation'? In what areas of your own life do you see opportunities to be a minister of reconciliation to others?
- What is the relationship between truth telling – to others, to God and to ourselves – and the work of reconciliation?
- How does the sacrament of reconciliation – through truthful confession, active listening, penance, forgiveness and the inseparable connection of relationship to God and one another it upholds – model the work of reconciliation and justice in the wider world?

Further reading

Colin E. Gunton (ed.), 2003, *The Theology of Reconciliation*, London: T&T Clark.
John Milbank, 2003, *Being Reconciled: Ontology and Pardon*, London: Routledge.
Pope John Paul II, 1984, *Reconciliation and Penance* [post-synodical apostolic exhortation], Vatican: Libreria Editrice Vaticana.

9

Love in Politics: An Invitation to a Public Faith

SIMON CUFF

There are two things you are not supposed to talk about in polite company: religion and politics. If you are religious, you are not supposed to meddle in the business of politics at all. Whenever a Christian makes a public intervention on behalf of the poor in line with the witness of Scripture, they are over-stepping their rightful religious terrain.

Not only are these statements false, they are all political statements. This chapter spells out some of the contours of Christian political witness and the vision of society that we have as a Church. It explores how we as Christians can live as an offering of Christ's love in the public square. In doing so, we will look at some examples of Christian political inter-vention and the contours of a Christian political contribution to public life.

The Church and politics

The Church has a vision of abundant life for each and every person. As Christians with a vision for the life of every person in society, to say that the Church should not articulate that vision is itself a political statement. It serves to silence the potential critique of the status quo articulated by the Church's vision for society. To assert that the Church must keep silent in the face of injustice, poverty and the structures and mechanisms in society which give rise to such poverty and injustice suggests that it is possible to maintain political neutrality on such issues. But this political neutrality is a myth.

Each and every statement about society either commends or critiques the status quo, and therefore every such statement is political. It seeks either to maintain or to transform the status quo. The Church ever asks whether the status quo is serving the Christian vision of society. This means always asking whether society's status quo is serving each and every one of those who are created in God's image – that is all of us. While the Church remains neutral in relation to particular politicians or political parties, it cannot be neutral in commending or critiquing the political vision of a particular politician or Party. The Church cannot be neutral in offering her commendation or critique and putting forward her own political vision.

One of the most significant examples of Christian political intervention is that of the former Archbishop of Canterbury, William Temple. His *Christianity and Social Order* published in 1942 set out a vision for society in post-war Britain. His vision for society was hugely influential and contributed to the post-war consensus which governed British political life for the remainder of the century. *Christianity and Social Order* repeatedly tackles the claim that the Church has no right to speak out on political and economic problems, with chapter headings including 'What Right has the Church to interfere?', 'How should the Church interfere?', 'Has the Church claimed to intervene before?' Such intervention, Temple insists, is not anything new. He points to the long history of Church inter-vention in and contribution to the public square. He then goes on to set out a method for the Church to offer such political interventions. Temple's method for Christian involvement in politics is to proclaim the points where existing social order is in conflict with Christ's kingdom of mercy and love and to go about the task of reshaping that existing social order to con-form to that kingdom. Central to this is the encouragement for all Christians to play their part in proclaiming and contributing to the Church's task in their daily lives.

It is impossible for the Church to remain politically neutral, because we know that God does not remain neutral in the face of injustice. The Church is unable to divide society into areas where God is interested and areas where God is not interested, labelling them the 'religious' and the 'political'. Such a division into religious and political realms fosters a false separation of the spiritual and the material that is contrary to genuine Christian belief. Christianity is not some sort of escapism from daily life, but rather a call to live life in all its fullness even here and now. At the heart of the Christian faith is not only that God refuses to retreat from the world but that God actually enters into it and lives within our social and political life as one of us. It's what we call the incarnation of Jesus Christ. God in Christ speaks and even lives into the material and political realms of our life, and so we cannot pretend as if we're free to be neutral on matters of injustice if we are to follow Christ.

Two cities

Our word 'politics' derives from the Greek *polis*, meaning 'city'. 'Politics' are the affairs of the city. The polis as a city is not a geographical or legal entity but the inhabitants or 'citizens' of each particular city. Politics is about the common affairs of public life. It's about the lives of those who make up the polis.

Christian thought is no stranger to visions of the justly ordered city which God will bring about. Both the letter to the Hebrews and the book of Revelation look forward to the heavenly city which God is preparing for the faithful (Heb. 11.10; 12.22; 13.14; Rev. 3.12; 21.2—22.5). The future heavenly city has been an inspiration for many different forms of Christian political witness across the centuries forming earthly society in anticipation of the new heaven and the new earth.

The Christian's primary obligation is to the heavenly city. This is not controversial and is the central argument of one of the most significant works of theology, St Augustine's *City of God*. Augustine divides between the earthly city and the heavenly city, identifying Christians as strangers in the earthly city, pilgrims towards the eternal heavenly city for which they are destined. However, this does not mean that the Christian has no vision for just action within the earthly polis. Elsewhere, for example, Augustine notes the respective duties of the rich and the poor regarding the common good: 'you rich, lay out your money; you poor refrain from plundering. You rich distribute your means, you poor bridle your desires' (Augustine, *Sermon 85*).

The common good

The common good is a central feature of Christian political thought. The common good requires the Christian to seek not only their own welfare but the good of every member of the society of which they are a part: 'seek the welfare of the city where I have sent you ... for in its welfare you will find your welfare' (Jer. 29.7). The common good reminds Christians that the welfare of the individual and the welfare of the whole are intimately connected. If an individual or section of society is in suffering, the common good demands attempts be made to alleviate that suffering. Policies that benefit one section of society at the expense of another, or without addressing the suffering of individuals or other sections of society, are a violation of this common good.

As Christians, the common good also implies a particular attitude towards material property or 'goods'. There are Scriptural indications of common ownership among Christians (e.g. Acts 2.44; 4.32). Until the modern era, the prevailing consensus held that goods were intended by God for common or universal ownership, with private stewardship the best means of distribution of these goods. For example, St Ambrose writes against the accumulation of goods for one's self: 'You are not making a gift of what is yours to the poor man, but you are giving him back what is his. You have been appropriating things that are meant to be for the common use of everyone. The earth belongs to everyone, not to the rich' (Ambrose, *On Naboth* 12.53). St Thomas Aquinas outlines the benefits of private stewardship in encouraging production of goods, avoiding confusion and limiting disputes so that one 'ought to possess external things, not as his own, but as common, so that, to wit, he is ready to communicate them to others in their need' (Aquinas, *Summa Theologica* 2.2.66). The common good implies the need to ask searching questions about the 'goods' we own, our stewardship of them, our readiness 'to communicate them to others in their need' and what God is asking of us by entrusting us with them.

The common good draws our attention to those around us, those with whom we share our society and ultimately our planet. To live as a Christian in the world is to live as a pilgrim towards the heavenly city which will be our eternal home. However, as Christians, living in the earthly cities and other communities we call home, we have a duty to love those whom we live alongside. Christian politics is based on this love of neighbour and the network of relationships in which we find ourselves as human beings. This is especially true of those pushed out of the polis or to the margins of society. Christ is executed as a common criminal outside the gates of the city (John 19.20) ever alerting us to those whom society persecutes or rejects.

The practical requirements of the love of neighbour recognize the fundamental human dignity of each and every human being. Catholic Social Teaching – the social doctrine of the Roman Catholic Church – represents a significant tradition of Christian political thought. From its outset with Pope Leo XIII's publication of *Rerum Novarum* in 1891, this tradition has recognized that the protection and promotion of human dignity is the basis of what it means for a Christian to act justly in the world. So, for example, in 1931 Pope Pius XI refers to the 'sacred rights of workers that flow from their dignity as men [sic] and Christians' (*Quadragesimo Anno* 28). This dignity is based on the creation of each and every human in the image of God (Gen. 1.26–27).

The protection and promotion of human dignity because of our creation in the image of God requires naming those places and situations of injustice where human dignity is not being preserved. As Christians we have a duty to observe the reality of our social situations and alert the world to the existence of injustice wherever it occurs. We have a duty to observe society as it really is and to confront any injustice which damages the dignity of our fellow human beings.

St Oscar Romero: a witness

St Oscar Romero (1917–80) was a model for Christian political engagement, and the potential costliness of Christian witness in the political sphere. Romero became Archbishop of San Salvador during the period leading up to the Salvadoran Civil War between the military government and a coalition of left-wing groups. This period saw the murder and disappearance of many as part of a campaign of intimidation. In this context, Romero was forced to confront the relationship between the Church and politics. This confrontation led ultimately to his martyrdom.

As he became increasingly aware of the injustices and violations of human dignity occurring around him, Romero dwelt increasingly on the role of the Church in relation to politics. His four pastoral letters sent as Archbishop demonstrate this trend. For Romero, the Church has a duty to denounce injustice, and 'the Church has also to denounce what has rightly been called structural sin: those social, economic, cultural, and political structures that effectively drive the majority of our people onto the margins of society. When the Church hears the cry of the oppressed she cannot but denounce the social structures that give rise to and perpetuate the misery from which the cry arises' (Romero, pp. 10–11). He goes further, noting that 'just as injustice takes concrete forms, so the promotion of justice must take concrete forms. It should come as a surprise to no one that the Church encourages particular methods of achieving justice' (p. 11).

Romero notes that this proclamation of justice is for both the rich and the poor. It means liberating the rich from the dehumanizing idolatry of wealth, and the poor from the dehumanizing marginalization of poverty: 'To those who had become dehumanized because of their desire for profits, [Jesus] clearly demonstrated, through his love, how to recover their lost human dignity; with the poor, dehumanized because pushed to the margins of society, he sat at table, also out of love, to bring hope back to them' (p. 13).

This is an integral part of the Church's mission, according to Romero, despite the costliness of this mission: 'if the Church is faithful to her mission of denouncing the sin that brings misery to many, and if she proclaims her hope for a more just, humane world, then she is persecuted and calumniated, she is branded as subversive and communist' (p. 13). Romero points out here how the Church's intervention on behalf of the poor and marginalized is often dismissed as being politically biased or left-wing. The 1986 Church of England report on urban poverty, *Faith in the City*, for example, was dismissed as 'pure marxist' and 'communist' (Glover, p. 30). Such criticism is an attempt to silence the Church from adding its voice to those whose voices society struggles to hear. Romero notes such criticism stems from those with power not wanting anybody to defend those who lack power or agency.

In the face of such criticism, Romero highlights the distinction between the Church's mission and all political philosophies. In his final homily in San Salvador cathedral he insisted that the Church cannot be identified with any one political movement or party. For Romero, the central task of the Church is a prophetic one – to proclaim and denounce.

But merely proclaiming justice and denouncing injustice will not be enough. We need to understand Romero carefully here. He is not simply calling for a Christian political witness which stands shouting from the sidelines. The Church's prophetic proclamation and denunciation involves the Church's support for, and participation in, practical efforts to transform situations of injustice. Martin Luther King describes this role in reflecting on the early Church: 'The Church was not merely a thermometer that recorded the ideas and principles of popular opinion; it was a thermostat that transformed the mores of society. Wherever the early Christians entered a town the power structure got disturbed' (King, p. 14).

Nationalism and taxation: two examples

The Church's prophetic proclamation and denunciation looks towards the political transformation of injustice in society. This means denouncing situations or attitudes which promote injustice, and lending support for practical means of achieving justice in society. We can take the examples of nationalism and taxation as two areas where the Church sets forth its vision for society in terms which have practical consequences for our public life.

Nationalism involves the absolutizing of an idea of one's own nation. Nationalists put their nation, or their conception of their nation, above the demands or interests of other nations and even individuals within their nation who do not fit their conception. Often nationalism sees the construction of national myths which themselves unjustly exclude particular people or peoples from the nationalist's account of their society. This is not to be confused with patriotism, which sees justifiable pride in the contribution your particular society has made and can make to human society as a whole.

Nationalism represents a risk to the common good when a nation puts its own interest first and at odds with wider interest of relations between nations and across the human family. Each human being is a member not only of a national community, but the wider human community. Indeed, divides between people groups were exactly what Christ came to overcome (Rom. 10.12; Gal. 3.28; Eph. 2.14).

If denouncing pernicious forms of nationalism offers one example of something the Church denounces in her political witness, the role of taxation is one example of where the Church can speak out in favour of justice. Few of us relish paying tax. We often hear that we should pay our taxes because Jesus said, 'give to the emperor the things that are the emperor's, and to God the things that are God's' (Mark 12.17 and parallels). This passage is often taken to suggest there are respective religious and political realms. However, there is a deep irony here, which is important to our discussion at hand. We cannot divide what is God's from what is the emperor's because, properly speaking, everything is God's.

Modern systems of progressive taxation (where tax rates increase as taxable income increases) are an example of where the Church has spoken out in favour of a policy it sees as just and contributing to the common good. An example of this is the 1986 report of the United States Catholic Bishops' Conference: *Economic Justice for All*. The Bishops commend progressive taxation as a means to fulfil the demands of basic justice and overcoming the inequitable concentration of privilege in a wealthy few (§76). They argue that any tax system should be guided by three principles: 1) raise adequate revenues to pay for public need, especially basic needs of the poor; 2) be progressive, so that those with relatively greater financial resources pay a higher rate as a means to reduce 'the severe inequalities of income and wealth'; and 3) the poorest/lowest should avoid tax altogether. They insist that the 'tax system should be continually evaluated in terms of its impact on the poor' (§202).

The biblical witness in favour of paying taxes is less about taxation and more about identity. The temple tax was a half-shekel payment made by all adult males. Women and men could pay voluntarily, but pagans and Samaritans could not. The biblical basis for the temple tax is found in Exodus 30.14: 'Each one who is registered, from twenty years old and upwards, shall give the Lord's offering'. Fundamentally this tax is about identity, who belongs to the people of God. In Matthew's Gospel, the possible implication that early Christians should continue paying the temple tax (Matt. 17.24–27) suggests that they should continue to identify themselves with God's people in paying the temple tax.

Above all, taxation is about identity. It is about who we are as Christians and what kind of society we want to live in and the kind of people we want to be. Progressive taxation is an important means of asserting and enabling a society in which wealth is held across society with a view especially to using the fruits of taxation in service of those who benefit most from the social investment taxation enables. Namely, the poor.

Preferential option for the poor

This brings us to the final ingredient of our introduction to Christian political witness: the place of the poor. Any Christian political intervention is marked by its awareness of and focus on the poor. The incarnation is heralded as the ultimate reminder of God's preference for the poor: 'He has brought down the powerful from their thrones, and lifted up the lowly' (Luke 1.52). God's incarnation as one of us is God's eternal pledge of preference for the poor. In Christ, God takes on our poverty so that we might all become rich (2 Cor. 8.9).

From the very beginning of the history of the Church, this focus on the poor is essential. Paul's mission is recognized by the Apostles and he is told to 'remember the poor' (Gal. 2.10). We are alerted to our duty towards the poor and the marginalized. The parable of the rich man and Lazarus (Luke 16.19–31) reminds us of our need to be aware of the poor man at our gate, and be attentive to the suffering of our neighbour. In Luke's Gospel, Jesus is clear: 'Blessed are you who are poor, for yours is the kingdom of God' (Luke 6.20).

Again and again, Scripture reminds us to be attentive to those in need. This need for attentiveness has been described as the 'preferential option for the poor'. This phrase is derived from liberation theology, but as the liberation theologian Gustavo Gutiérrez notes: 'In English, the word merely connotes a choice between two things. In Spanish, however, it evokes the sense of commitment. The option for the poor is not optional, but is incumbent upon every Christian. It is not something that a Christian can either take or leave' (Hartnet). It might be better translated as the preferential obligation for the poor.

The Church's political witness is always directed towards the poorest in society. The reason for the Church's focus on the poor is not only because the poor are deserving objects of charity, but because the poor are always with us as a reminder of the demands of justice in whatever polis we happen to find ourselves. The Church's focus is not only on those who are poor and in need of charity, but the reason for their poverty and the mechanisms in society which give rise to the affront on their dignity which poverty necessarily brings about.

The Church, in her mission to point towards the eternal city which is our heavenly home, ever sets herself against the structures which give rise to the marginalization and poverty of those who are poor. The poor are not merely present in society as recipients of charity, but as a sign of where society at large is failing in its commitment to the common good. This necessitates a political involvement on the part of the Christian. Pope Francis describes this best: 'involvement in politics is an obligation for a Christian. We Christians cannot "play the role of Pilate", washing our hands of it; we cannot. We must be involved in politics because politics is one of the highest forms of charity for it seeks the Common Good' (Pope Francis, 'Address'). The Church in her political witness focuses her attention on the poor, because the alleviation of the structures and mechanisms which give rise to poverty are the best means to ensure the promotion of justice and to signpost the heavenly city which is our home.

Questions for further reflection

- The life and teachings of Jesus do not hesitate to show God's preferential love for the poor. What does this teach us about God's love for the whole world? How does it shape our love towards others?
- So much of our lives today – the decisions we make, even our desires and longings – revolve around consumption, possession and ownership. How might the teaching of Scripture that we are not owners but stewards critique our society and call us to change in our own lives?
- What does it mean to say that we can never live politically neutral lives? How might that affect our perspective and activity in our communities and relationships?

Bibliography

D. Glover, 2011, *Turbulent Priests: The Archbishop of Canterbury in Contemporary English Politics*, London: Theos.

Pope Francis, 7 June 2013, 'Address of Pope Francis to the Students of Jesuit Schools in Italy and Albania', at http://www.vatican.va/con tent/francesco/en/speeches/2013/june/documents/papa-francesco_ 20130607_scuole-gesuiti.html (accessed 23.8.2019).

D. Hartnett, 3 Febuary 2003, 'Remembering the Poor': Interview with Gustavo Gutiérrez', in *America Magazine*, https://www.america magazine.org/faith/2003/02/03/remembering-poor-interview-gustavo-Gutiérrez (accessed 28.82018).

Martin Luther King, Jr, 1968, *Letter from Birmingham Jail*, Stanford: Overbrook Press.

Pius XI, *Quadragesimo Anno 28, May 15, 1931*, http://www.vatican.va/ content/pius-xi/en/encyclicals/documents/hf_p-xi_enc_19310515_ quadragesimo-anno.html (accessed 22.8.2019).

Oscar Romero, 1977, *The Church, the Body of Christ in History: Second Pastoral Letter of Archbishop Romero*, http://www.romero trust.org.uk/sites/default/files/second%20pastoral%20letter.pdf (accessed 28.8.2019).

United States Catholic Bishops' Conference, 1986, *Economic Justice for All: Pastoral Letter on Catholic Social Teaching and the U.S. Economy*, http://www.usccb.org/upload/economic_justice_for_all.pdf (accessed 28.8.2019).

Further reading

Luke Bretherton, 2019, *Christ and the Common Life: Political Theology and the Case for Democracy*, Grand Rapids: Eerdmans.

Malcolm Brown (ed.), 2014, *Anglican Social Theology: Renewing the Vision Today*, London: Church House Publishing.

Simon Cuff, 2019, *Love in Acton: Catholic Social Teaching for Every Church*, London: SCM Press.

Anthony Reddie, 2019, *Theologising Brexit: A Liberationist and Post-colonial Critique*, Abingdon: Routledge.

Anna Rowlands, 2021, *Towards a Politics of Communion: Catholic Social Teaching in Dark Times*, London: Bloomsbury.

Stephen Spencer (ed.), 2018, *Theology Reforming Society: Revisiting Anglican Social Theology*, London: SCM Press.

Samuel Wells, David Barclay and Russell Rook, 2017, *For Good: The Church and the Future of Welfare*, London: Canterbury Press.

10

Love in Hospitality:
An Invitation to Welcome

JENNIFER STRAWBRIDGE

What is hospitality?

When you search for the meaning of 'hospitality' online, images of glasses of wine, plates of food and cups of tea dominate. Hospitality in our culture is closely linked both with a profession of hosting and catering and with the act of welcoming someone into our home. Hospitality is familiar. Hospitality is privilege. Hospitality connects us with one another.

So what then do we mean when we say that hospitality lies at the heart of our faith? Certainly conversations of faith and life take place over meals and beverages of all kinds. Part of hospitality is about welcome and shared meals – as Jesus himself demonstrates time and again – but this is not the only kind of hospitality of which Scripture speaks or that we are called to practise as Christians. The very root of the word 'hospitality' in the New Testament makes this clear.

The word for 'hospitality' found in the New Testament – in Romans, 1 Timothy, Titus, Hebrews and 1 Peter – literally translates as 'love of stranger'. The word is *philoxenia* (*philos* being 'love' and *xeno* being 'stranger') and is the opposite of xenophobia.[1] Thus, hospitality in Scripture isn't simply about inviting a friend over for a cup of tea or a meal; it is not about the familiar. Hospitality is about the love of the other, the stranger, and the transformation that such love inevitably creates. As the great spiritual writer Henri Nouwen concludes, hospitality is 'the creation of a free space where the stranger can enter and become a friend instead of an enemy. Hospitality is not to change people, but to offer them space where change can take place. It is not to bring men and women over to our side, but to offer freedom not disturbed by dividing lines' (Nouwen, p. 68).

This understanding of hospitality in terms of love means that acts of hospitality cannot be separated from the God who is love (1 John 4.7–8). Not surprisingly, the connection between hospitality and the divine permeates the world in which Jesus and his followers lived. Ancient Greeks thought of Zeus as a special protector of strangers and guests and 'as patron deity of hospitality' (Keener, p. 2416). As such, extending hospitality to another was essential to showing one's devotion to the gods.

The God that Christians worship as Father, Son and Holy Spirit is also deeply connected with hospitality. We are created in the image of a relational God. Through God's love, we are welcomed into God's infinite triune life and because of the gift of hospitality that God gives to us, we are called to extend this same welcome to others. Discussions within the New Testament about standards of behaviour for a Christian, there-fore, often turn to the language of hospitality. Near the end of his letter to the Romans, Paul exhorts the community to 'let love be genuine', to 'love one another with mutual affection', and to 'extend hospitality to strangers' (Rom. 12.9, 10, 13). Likewise, the author of 1 Timothy writes that 'whoever aspires to the office of bishop' (1 Tim. 3.1–2) needs to be 'hospitable' and the author of Titus writes that appointed 'elders' 'must be hospitable' (Titus 1.5, 8). In each of these texts, the love and call of God is intimately connected with hospitality.

That Scripture commands time and again that we be kind to strangers, however, suggests that we're not very good at practising hospitality. We also forget all too easily that we are in need of love and welcome and that we are often strangers in this world. In Exodus 22.21, for example, God reminds God's people not to oppress a stranger or alien, reminding them that 'you were aliens in the land of Egypt'. Similarly, Leviticus 19 commands God's people not to oppress the alien or stranger in the land – that this needs to be said suggests it was happening – for they should 'love the alien as yourself' and remember that 'you were aliens' as well (Lev. 19.33–34). Whether we readily admit it or not, most of us are drawn to people like us. But Scripture repeatedly reminds us not only to love brother and sister, but also to love the stranger, the alien, the outsider, the exile. We are, as those called by God, to love and to welcome whoever we find to be stranger, alien and excluded because of race or class or colour or physical limitation or gender or sexual identity. Hospitality is an essential part of the so-called 'golden rule' to do to others as you would have them do to you (Matt. 7.12).

Throughout the Gospels, Jesus is the primary example of this barrier-destroying hospitality. Encountered as host and as guest, Jesus embodies hospitality. He breaks bread with his disciples, with known sinners and with those at the highest and lowest ends of ancient society. Jesus' stories or parables draw on images of hospitality – of banquet tables, dinners, feasts and the sharing of food and drink – to tell his followers something about what the kingdom of God is like. Jesus' example as host and guest, offering welcome and his very self, is the model for the hospitality we are called to offer. As he makes clear in Matthew 25, whatever we do to the 'least of these', which includes the welcoming of the stranger (Matt. 25.35), we do it to Jesus. But what does this look like in practice?

The practice of hospitality

As we've already touched on in this chapter, Scripture gives us a number of excellent examples to help us understand what hospitality looks like in practice. Here, we'll look at a few of those examples: Genesis 18, Matthew 25 and Luke 24 and 1 Peter 4.

Genesis 18: the Trinity

Perhaps the greatest example of hospitality in ancient Jewish tradition is the story of Abraham and Sarah offering food, water and rest to messengers from God in Genesis 18. Within this story, three strangers appear to Abraham and Sarah. These strangers are never identified by name and in some places in this story, rather confusingly, are referred to in the singular and as 'the Lord'. Abraham offers them water to wash their feet, he prepares a meal for them with the help of Sarah, and he gives them a place for rest. In the course of their stay, the messengers tell Abraham and Sarah that God will give them a son, which comes as a complete surprise since Sarah is barren and is an older woman. Within this story of hospitality, strangers are welcomed and Abraham and Sarah are blessed.

In Christian writings, the story from Genesis 18 is mentioned in Hebrews 13.2 which tells its readers not to 'neglect to show hospitality to strangers, for by doing that some have entertained angels without knowing it' (the word for angel means 'messenger'). The story of Abraham's hospitality is also depicted in one of the world's most famous icons by Russian icon painter Andrei Rublev. The icon, in which three angels sit in a circle and represent the one God in three persons, is known both as *The Hospitality of Abraham* and *The Trinity*. Here, the image of the Trinity is interwoven with an image of hospitality, offering a concrete picture of our earlier discussion on hospitality's foundation in the life and love of God. 1 John 4.19 tells us that 'We love because he first loved us' and just as the love of God is reciprocal, so too is hospitality. The blessing offered is given and received by host and guest. Here, hospitality isn't about inviting a friend over for a cup of tea, though it can absolutely be that, it is connected to the very life of God.

This connection between hospitality and the Trinity is significant because within Christian tradition, Trinity is a foundation of relationship and community. The three persons of the Trinity are eternally united with one another in love. Father, Son and Holy Spirit are completely equal and yet possess a unique dignity and identity. The deepest mystery of the Trinity is that this dynamic relationship of God as Father, Son and Spirit and the outpouring of love from this relationship is the foundation for the Christian life. So it is no wonder that the Trinity is a firm foundation for hospitality. The Trinity describes the relationship we are called to have with one another and with all of creation in its most perfect form (Strawbridge, p. 16). The Trinity is at the heart of community and of perfect hospitality. The model of Abraham, Sarah and the three messengers reveals that hospitality is not simply something we offer as individuals. It is something that we also do as community, especially when that community can help us to love those we struggle to love, welcome those we struggle to welcome, and include those we prefer to exclude. This story from Genesis 18 and the depiction of the three messengers as the Trinity teach and challenge us in how to live and love and imitate God in Christ by the power of the Spirit. True hospitality – truly welcoming a stranger – is hard work but time and again in Scripture we are told that in welcoming the stranger we are welcoming God.

Abraham and Sarah offered hospitality and were blessed, and while we don't know that they might not have been blessed in some other way had they refused to welcome the three strangers, the story does suggest that the blessing is dependent on the welcome given. The link between love of stranger – providing rest and sustenance – and God's blessing is significant; the two in this story are inseparable. The same is true in the hospitality we are called to offer as Christians, though, as we discover in the next example, the blessing we are promised is direct encounter with Christ.

Matthew 25 and Luke 24: Jesus

The idea that in welcoming a stranger we welcome God is made especially clear not only in Genesis 18 and its interpretation and reception in Rublev's icon, but also by Jesus himself. In many places the Gospels explicitly connect hospitality with encountering Jesus, including Jesus's parable of the sheep and goats in Matthew 25 and the post-resurrection story on the Emmaus Road in Luke 24.

Jesus's parable in Matthew 25 is one of many stories that Matthew tells about judgement. In brief, according to Jesus, at the end of time the king will divide sheep and goats, the former to receive everlasting life and reward and the latter to endure eternal fire and punishment. Both the sheep and the goats will be judged on the same criteria, which includes feeding the hungry, clothing the naked, caring for the sick and welcoming the stranger, all of which offer opportunities for direct encounter with Christ. But this is not simply a checklist of the things a Christian must do in order to gain eternal life. Welcoming the stranger, hospitality, isn't something we offer superficially in order to tick a box to get to heaven. Rather, hospitality, just like all of the other actions described by Jesus, demands our full buy-in, it requires relationship and it makes us vulnerable.

The action of hospitality found in this 'list' involves vulnerability and relationship as it asks us to open ourselves and even our homes to a stranger, something which is both risky and exposing. Strangers are, by definition, not people we know. Strangers are strange. And we don't always engage well with those who are different from us. So when Jesus says that by welcoming the stranger the sheep have welcomed Christ, we might think this sounds lovely and sweet. But we have to remember that throughout his life, Christ crosses every social and economic boundary. In his expansive and unconditional love for all – sinner and saint – he does what we rarely can.

Furthermore, Jesus is pretty clear in this parable that the welcome given to a stranger isn't something that we necessarily know that we're doing. In this parable, the sheep didn't know they were doing something right any more than the goats knew they were doing something wrong. The sheep and goats seem equally puzzled by their fate and both ask: when was it that you, Jesus, were a stranger and we welcomed you? Jesus tells the sheep he is grateful for all they did to nourish, welcome, clothe, tend to and be with him. But they cannot ever recall doing any of these things for Jesus. And the goats cannot recall ever seeing Jesus anywhere, much less in need of anything. As their sentences are handed down, both groups respond the same: we didn't know we would be judged for that. They are not judged on their church tradition or religious practices or their theology. The only criterion for judgement in this story is how they responded to the need of their neighbours, of the stranger and of the world around them. They are judged by how they responded to those deemed to be less worthy of love.

The call to hospitality, to welcome and love the stranger, offers infinite opportunities to encounter Christ in our lives, and the key element in this parable is that Jesus is here, now, among us always as the stranger, as the one excluded, waiting for us to pay attention. This is the one thing that the sheep do and the goats do not. The sheep stop, listen, and see and seek Christ in the other. The sheep model hospitality for us.

Luke 24 offers another model of hospitality, also directly connected with encountering Christ, in the story of two disciples walking along the Emmaus Road. They are grieving deeply as they return home from Jerusalem after witnessing the crucifixion and death of Jesus, their Lord. They are joined on their journey by a man they do not recognize who listens to them and shares the scriptures with them. Only when they insist that this stranger stay with them for a meal – only when they offer hospitality to the stranger – are their eyes opened leading them to understand that the stranger with them on the road has been Jesus all along.

Even in the place of confusion and despair, the risen Lord walked alongside the disciples as stranger and friend. Even in those moments when they didn't and couldn't recognize God in their midst and their lives, God was with them. Only in the act of hospitality, only as they broke bread together, did they recognize Jesus. Like the story of the sheep and the goats, this story reminds us once again that God is with us and that when we extend welcome to the stranger, we welcome God. Both stories reveal that we never know when and where we will encounter God in our lives, grace in our lives, love in our lives. But they also make clear that we are called to offer this love and this grace to others, even the oblivious stranger on the road who seems to be the only person in Jerusalem who doesn't know that Jesus just died.

The story of the road to Emmaus brings us back as well to the importance of community in acts of hospitality. None of us can endure the changes and chances of this world alone and God comes alongside us in the midst of life's challenges and welcomes us, offering sustenance and presence. Both of these gospel stories remind us that God is in the fellow strangers on the road, inviting us all to a banquet where there is room for everyone. Hospitality isn't restricted, and it's not about showing off how much we have or how warm our beds are. Hospitality is about encountering Christ in the other, so that they, in turn, may encounter Christ in us. Hospitality in this sense is transformative and may even save someone's life.

This latter point was made clear to me in a conversation about hospitality not long ago with a colleague from India. He was clear that hospitality was a matter of life or death for many Indian Christians undergoing targeted persecution in recent decades. He could tell numerous stories of people who took in strangers who were Christians in order to hide them from violent attackers. The risk of such hospitality was immense. Taking in a stranger in this volatile climate exposed the host to the same violent mobs should anyone find out they were harbouring a Christian. And the guest – the stranger welcomed – also placed their life in the hands of a stranger in whose home they were now hiding. The action was literally lifesaving and transforming for the Christian and their family and in the process, it changed both guest and host. By offering a safe space for strangers, the identity of the strangers – both guest and host – transformed as the other was known.

With this story, we understand a bit more not only why the word for 'hospitality' in the New Testament means 'love of stranger', but we also begin to grasp why the root of the English word shares the same Latin root as hospice and hospital. Within the ancient world, these were places that were safe for rest. Monasteries often took on the role of hospital or hospice as a place of safe lodging and the Rule of St Benedict includes a quotation from Matthew 25 in the instruction that 'All guests who present themselves are to be welcomed as Christ, for he himself will say "I was a stranger and you welcomed me"' (§53.1). In the Old City of Jerusalem today, many English-speaking visitors and pilgrims are surprised to see so many signs for hospitals and hospices in the city, without often realizing that they are places of lodging and sustenance (and, as a monk friend once shared with me, the best hot chocolate in the Old City). They are places of hospitality, living out still today the examples we find in Matthew and Luke.

1 Peter 4: the stranger and exile

When we think about hospitality in the letter of 1 Peter, we first have to realize that this letter is addressed to those who are aliens, exiles and strangers. The communities encouraged by this letter are persecuted by and excluded from society because they have been chosen by God and identify as God's people. For many in wider society, this makes them strange (and therefore strangers). The act of God that chooses and includes those who are exiles and aliens is the same act that excludes those chosen within their cultural context. God's action is the basis for inclusion and yet those included are, by virtue of this inclusion, excluded from their world. With this as a foundation, the author of 1 Peter plays with the language of *xenos* or stranger/alien/other, writing to people who are strangers in this world while at the same time encouraging them to offer hospitality (1 Peter 4.9).

This call to offer hospitality is, for 1 Peter, the way one imitates Christ and answers the call to follow Christ, which we saw spelled out in the previous section. But in this call, especially to a people who are displaced in the world, 1 Peter also picks up on the power dynamics inherent in hospitality. Those who are strangers are vulnerable, and those who offer hospitality have significant power through this act of welcome and love. The one who loves the stranger has the power to transform the stranger into someone who is no longer strange. Once known and once loved, neither guest nor host is stranger to the other.

1 Peter also recognizes something touched on in the previous section about the risk that accompanies hospitality. By definition, the stranger is unknown and extending hospitality – literally love – to an unknown person is risky and demands vulnerability on the part of the one extending that love. Loving and welcoming a stranger makes the one who loves and welcomes vulnerable. Inclusion is not without risk. Perhaps this helps us better understand why Jesus faced so much hostility when he shared a meal with others, when he offered and received hospitality. Not everyone is comfortable with the risk inherent in loving and welcoming someone who is unknown and thus the reaction to this love can range from awe to revulsion.

Perhaps here it is worth mentioning that 1 Peter calls for hospitality to be exercised in a particular way, reminding the Christian that what the world thinks about their action towards another doesn't ultimately matter. In 1 Peter 4, hospitality is simply to be enacted without grumbling. That such a clarification is needed suggests that hospitality was being offered, but with grumbling. Even the earliest followers of Christ had bad days and demanding guests. But even so, they are reminded that as strangers in the world themselves, they are called to welcome the other; strangers are called to welcome strangers. In a world often fearful of strangers – remember the opposite of the word for hospitality here is xenophobia – this can be a difficult task. The difficulty increases when we realize that in this context, the Christian is stranger as well. This sits uncomfortably, especially in a world telling us that we need to be popular and encouraging us to be with the 'in' crowd. Nothing in our world tells us that being strange or stranger is cool; most children now grow up learning about 'stranger danger'. So this language of 1 Peter to love the stranger without grumbling challenges us. And rightly so.

Hospitality, as you've picked up by this point, is a call from
God, and offering hospitality, truly loving that which we deem
strange, is not something many of us do instinctively. Our
world tells us not to. But God tries time and again to draw us
back to God's heart, back to God's love, and part of that love
is the community of God's people. The wonderful thing about
this community is that we don't create it, nor do we have the
authority or the power as individuals to determine who is 'in'
the people of God and who is not. That's up to God. Rather
than setting boundaries, drawing lines and pronouncing judgement, we are called to cross boundaries, knock down dividing
walls, and love one another, and one of the ways we do that,
one of the primary ways we do that, is through hospitality. For
hospitality reminds us not only of our identity as God's chosen
people, strange and beloved in this world, but it calls us from
that place to love those who are strangers, who are on the
margins, who are excluded, who are suffering, who we might
deem unlovable. In Christ, there are no strangers. Hospitality is about creating community and drawing God's people
together into the heart of God.

Hospitality as foundation for Christian life

One interpretation of Rublev's icon of the Trinity and the hospitality of Abraham is that the perspective of the icon invites
the person engaging it to the table. Within the icon, the place
at the table closest to the viewer is vacant and the three persons
all sit, wings intertwined, looking back at the person looking
at them, and with their hands and gestures draw the viewer to
their place at the table. In a true embodiment of hospitality, the
icon invites all without discrimination to share the feast and to
a moment of rest. All are within the embrace of God's love and
this love is the love we offer in the act of hospitality. Such radical love and welcome doesn't mean that we will always agree
with those we are called to love and welcome. Hospitality
isn't the same as approval, but it is also not simply tolerance.

Tolerance is not love, but judgement. No one wants to be tolerated. Rather, the hospitality embodied across Scripture demands that love be genuine and without hypocrisy (Rom. 12.9; 1 Peter 1.22). Hospitality calls us deeper into community and draws us into relationship with all creation.

Such language of inclusion and radical welcome raises questions for Christian life and witness. How often do we look to Scripture to make decisions about how we might include or exclude the stranger who is different from us because of tradition or behaviour or being or identity? The call to hospitality, to love the stranger, tells us that we are asking the wrong question. Hospitality threatens and overturns our attempts at exclusion and division, especially when we realize how intimately connected hospitality is to the love of God and the love that God extends to us. The commands to love one another found across Scripture and to 'welcome one another … as Christ has welcomed you, for the glory of God' (Rom. 15.7) lie at the centre of the call of Christians to hospitality. The promise that we encounter Christ, welcome Christ, and love Christ when we welcome the stranger, is at the heart of our understanding of what it means when we proclaim 'God with us'. Christian hospitality challenges us to come to terms with our own identity as strangers in this world and calls us to step outside the comfort zones of our often narrow lives. This understanding of hospitality as a call to love makes this act one of the highest callings of the Christian life. Xenophobia has no place in the heart of God. For as Christians, we are called to philoxenia, to hospitality, to love of stranger.

Note

1 Philoxenia is also, one might argue, the opposite of the title given to the cyclops Polyphemus in Homer's *Odyssey* who was known not for providing food for his guest, but feasting on them, earning him the later title *xenodaites*, the one who devours strangers.

Questions for further reflection

- Jesus often extends acts of love to those who are at the margins and excluded from community. Who are the people we think of as being beyond the reach of God's love? Who have we written off, turned away from, discounted or ignored? Who would we find it difficult to welcome into our homes or to a seat at our table? How does the call to hospitality – to love the stranger – speak into these situations?
- Hospitality is a way of being and seeing the world so that strangers become friends and not enemies. What 'strangers' are in your world? Who in your world is feeling alienated, excluded or displaced? How might you extend hospitality to them?

Bibliography

Craig S. Keener, 2014, 'Hospitality', in *Acts: An Exegetical Commentary, Volume 3*, Grand Rapids: Baker Academic.

Henri J. M. Nouwen, 1975, *Reaching Out: The Three Movements of the Spiritual Life*, New York: Doubleday.

Jennifer Strawbridge, 2019, 'Love in Excess – God the Holy Trinity', in Jennifer Strawbridge, Jarred Mercer and Peter Groves (ed.), *Love Makes No Sense: An Invitation to Christian Theology*, London: SCM Press, pp. 12–22.

Further reading

Al Barrett and Ruth Harley, 2020, *Being Interrupted: Re-imagining the Church's Mission from the Outside, In*, London: SCM Press.

John Koenig, 2001, *New Testament Hospitality: Partnership with Strangers as Promise and Mission*, Eugene, OR: Wipf and Stock Publishers.

Jenn Strawbridge (ed.), 2020, *The First Letter of Peter: A Global Commentary*, London: SCM Press.

Tom Wilson, 2019, *Hospitality, Service, Proclamation: Interfaith Engagement as Christian Discipleship*, London: SCM Press.

Index of Names and Subjects